1 & 2 TIMOTHY & TITUS:

DISPENSATIONALLY CONSIDERED

A GRACE EXPOSITIONAL COMMENTARY

SECOND EDITION

DR. DAVID ALAN GREENE

GraceWord Publishing, LLC
www.gracewordpublishing.com
U.S.A.

GRACEWORD PUBLISHING

Contents

To My Grandsons Judah, Wyatt, and Ravi

Study to shew thyself approved unto God,
a workman that needeth not to be ashamed,
rightly dividing the word of truth.

- Apostle Paul

Acknowledgements

I would like to express my gratitude to Jon and Susan McMahon for their continued encouragement, and a special thanks to Barbara Pennington and Frances Greene who worked together to proofread the manuscript.

Introduction

There is an approach to understanding Scripture that puts the entire Bible into a simple system of interpretation. The argument is that to understand God's Word we must reason from the general to the specific and not from the specific to the general. To choose any of Paul's epistles and read them apart from its biblical context would be looking at the specific outside the general structure of Scripture. This can get people into trouble.

God created a timeline and eternal plan for the restoration of His Creation. This plan was first mentioned in Genesis. It is known as the *protoevangelium* or the first announcement of good news. Genesis 3:15:

> 15 **And I will put enmity between thee and the woman, and between thy seed and <u>her seed</u>; it [her seed] shall bruise**

thy head, and thou shalt bruise his heel.

The word *seed* can be singular or plural. Here, it is singular and refers to *the Seed,* Who is Christ. Also, notice that it is the woman's seed because it was given to her by God. This is often called the *immaculate conception* or the divine impregnation of the virgin Mary with the holy *Seed.* Beginning with this very first promise of good news, there is a central theme throughout the Bible. It is said a scarlet thread is woven throughout Scripture. This Seed will redeem Creation!

God does things methodically as He works His plan of restoration. He makes Himself known to man through a series of progressive revelations. Paul has a student preacher named Timothy. The letters to both Timothy and Titus are referred to as the pastoral epistles because he is instructing them. Paul wants Timothy to understand and teach Scripture correctly so that he will not be ashamed or embarrassed. 2 Timothy 2:15:

> 15 **<u>Study to shew thyself approved</u> unto God, a workman that needeth not to be ashamed, <u>rightly dividing the word of truth.</u>**

The Greek word translated as *rightly dividing* is

orthotomeo. It is a compound word comprised of *ortho* which means *correct* or *with great precision. Tomeo* is a verb which means *to cut.* As examples, *orthodox* means *correct doctrine* while any medical procedure where something is removed uses in its name the suffix *-ectomy* (Gr. ek + tomeo) which means *to cut out.*

This concept of carefully dividing Scripture, when applied, makes a huge difference! As with most things, the Bible is the sum of its parts. These parts or divisions of the Bible are referred to as *dispensations.* In Greek, the word is *oikonomia.* It is also a compound word. It is comprised of *oikos* meaning *household* and *nomos* which means *law or rule.* Consider the present-day meaning of the word *administration.* A president rules or administrates the country by certain laws. Therefore, a *dispensation* is a period of time in which God *dispenses* or administrates His household.

A brief summary of the dispensations does not do the subject justice. I would recommend *Letters To Theophilus* which handles the subject in great detail. However, because it is critical to one's understanding the Bible, consider the following. Presently, we are in what some call the *Church Age.* However, I would not use this name because the word *church* has too many uses. I prefer the name *Age of Grace* because this is the very core of its message. Paul is the only one who uses the word *dispensation* in the Bible. It is used in the following verses:

1 Corinthians 9:17:

> 17 **For if I do this thing willingly, I have a reward: but if against my will, <u>a dispensation of the gospel is committed unto me.</u>**

Ephesians 1:10:

> 10 **That in <u>the dispensation of the fulness of times</u> he might gather together in one all things in Christ, both which are in heaven, and which are on earth; even [that is to say] in him:**

Ephesians 3:2:

> 2 **If ye have heard of <u>the dispensation of the grace of God</u> which is given me to you-ward [for you]:**

Colossians 1:25:

> 25 **Whereof I am made a minister, ac-**

cording to <u>the dispensation of God</u> which is given to me for you, to fulfil the word of God;

These verses should not be interpreted out of context but are only presented here as evidence of Paul's use of the word *dispensation.*

Many theologians have *carefully cut* or *rightly divided* the Bible into seven dispensations. It is the same as the number of days in Creation. Most critical for our purpose are two dispensations: the *Age of Law* and the *Age of Grace.* Under the Mosaic Covenant, Israel obligated itself to keeping the Law. The weight of which proved to be too much for them. The Gentiles, or non-Jews, were outside of this covenantal agreement. Following the Jews' rejection of their Messiah, in the last chapter of Acts, Paul makes a proclamation. Acts 28:28-29:

> 28 **Be it known therefore unto you, that <u>the salvation of God is sent unto the Gentiles</u>, and that <u>they will hear it</u>. 29 And when he had said these words, the Jews departed, and had great reasoning among themselves.**

The Apostle Paul wrote thirteen epistles or letters in the New Testament. Each letter was written to a group of believers or individuals such as Philemon, Titus, and Timothy. All of these letters, with the exception of Romans, were written to a group of people he knew personally. Many of them he lived with while teaching them face to face. Therefore, most recipients of these letters had a general understanding of Paul's doctrines before receiving his letter.

The letter to the Romans was different. Some believers had heard Paul and believed. Then, they relocated to the capitol city of Rome. Many who had not met or heard Paul teach had become believers through the testimony of others. Romans was written to provide a foundational basis of Paul's doctrine. Upon the substance of Romans are all his other letters written. Since it is a comprehensive summary of Pauline doctrine, it is placed first in the series of his epistles.

I like to use this as an example. Think about a multi-part series of some epic story. How difficult it would be to understand the full depth of a story by starting in the middle of season three? For this same reason, let us consider the basis of the unique gospel message which Paul preached. We must not confuse or combine his distinct message, the *Gospel of Grace,* with the message of the other twelve apostles. Paul made three missionary trips to proclaim his gospel.

His final trip was to Rome where he would be executed. Many of his later letters were written while he was a prisoner in Rome awaiting his trial.

The Apostle Paul preached a unique gospel message. Scripture confirms he personally received this from the Risen Savior. The information he received was a mystery and had never been disclosed to anyone until it was disclosed to him. We will see shortly that this gospel message was specifically directed to the Gentiles. We will start with the facts concerning his confrontation with the Risen Savior on the Road to Damascus. Acts 9:3-9:

> 3 And as he journeyed, he came near Damascus: and suddenly there shined round about him a light from heaven:
> 4 And he fell to the earth, and heard a voice saying unto him, Saul, Saul, why persecutest thou me? 5 And he said, Who art thou, Lord? And the Lord said, I am Jesus whom thou persecutest: it is hard for thee to kick against the pricks.
>
> 6 And he trembling and astonished said, Lord, what wilt thou have me to do? And the Lord said unto him, Arise, and go into the city, and it shall be told thee what thou must do.

7 And the men which journeyed with him stood speechless, hearing a voice, but seeing no man. **8** And Saul arose from the earth; and when his eyes were opened, he saw no man: but they led him by the hand, and brought him into Damascus.

9 And he was three days without sight, and neither did eat nor drink.

It is important for you to know that the Apostle Paul had never met Jesus during His earthly ministry. Therefore, he could not fulfill the requirements for the replacement of Judas as the twelfth apostle. (See Acts 1:21-26.)

God directs a faithful disciple named Ananias to heal Paul's blindness. Pay close attention to this dialogue between God and Ananias. Acts 9:10-16

10 And there was a certain disciple at Damascus, named Ananias; and to him said the Lord in a vision, Ananias. And he said, Behold, I am here, Lord. **11** And the Lord said unto him, Arise, and go into the street which is called Straight, and enquire in the house of Judas for one called Saul, of Tarsus: for, behold, he prayeth, 12 And hath seen in a vision a man named Ananias coming in, and putting his hand on him, that he might receive his sight.

13 Then Ananias answered, Lord, I have heard by many of this man, <u>how much evil he hath done to thy saints at Jerusalem</u>: 14 And here he hath authority from the chief priests to bind all that call on thy name.

15 But the Lord said unto him, <u>Go thy way: for he is a chosen vessel unto me, to bear my name before the Gentiles, and kings, and the children of Israel:</u> 16 <u>For I will shew him how great things he must suffer for my name's sake.</u>

In Paul's letter to the Galatians, he writes something he had most likely shared with other believers in person. These verses below recall his second meeting with the other apostles in Jerusalem. Paul had only met Peter and James once before on his previous trip and none of the others. Galatians 2:1-9:

1 Then fourteen years after I went up again to Jerusalem with Barnabas, and

took Titus with me also. 2 And I went up by revelation, and communicated unto them that gospel which I preach among the Gentiles, but privately to them which were of reputation, lest [for fear that] by any means I should run, or had run, in vain.

3 But neither Titus, who was with me, being a Greek, was compelled to be circumcised: 4 And that because of false brethren unawares brought in, who came in privily to spy out our liberty which we have in Christ Jesus, that they might bring us into bondage: 5 To whom we gave place by subjection, no, not for an hour; that the truth of the gospel might continue with you.

6 But of these who seemed to be somewhat [of importance], (whatsoever they were, it maketh no matter to me: God accepteth no man's person:) for they who seemed to be somewhat in conference added nothing to me:

7 But contrariwise, when they saw that the gospel of the uncircumcision was committed unto me, as the gospel of the

circumcision was unto Peter; 8 (For he that wrought effectually in Peter to the apostleship of the circumcision, the same was mighty in me toward the Gentiles:)

9 And when James, Cephas, and John, who seemed to be pillars, perceived the grace that was given unto me, they gave to me and Barnabas the right hands of fellowship; that we should go unto the heathen [Gentiles], and they unto the circumcision.

Paul provides a concise statement of this gospel in a letter to the Corinthians. Notice his use of the definite article *the* when referring to *the* gospel *wherein ye stand*. This is the basis of their salvation. 1 Corinthians 15:1-4:

1 Moreover, brethren, I declare unto you the gospel which I preached unto you, which also ye have received, and wherein ye stand; 2 By which also ye are saved, if ye keep in memory what I preached unto you, unless ye have believed in vain.

3 For I delivered unto you first of all that

which I also received, [1] how that Christ died for our sins according to the scriptures; 4 [2] And that he was buried, and [3] that he rose again the third day according to the scriptures:

We must see the simplicity of the *Gospel of Grace*. It consists of Christ's death on the Cross, His burial, and His resurrection. It is *the believing of these facts* which are the basis for our salvation. It is by His death, burial, and resurrection that we are *justified* or *proclaimed not guilty!* For in this, and in this alone, *Christ accomplished it all!*

The sufficiency of Christ's completed work on the Cross is critical and cannot be over emphasized. Nothing can be added. Paul makes this clear in all his letters. This is the most quoted of his verses. Ephesians 2:8-9:

8 For by grace are ye saved through faith; and that not of yourselves: it is the gift of God: 9 Not of works, lest [for fear that] any man should boast.

In his letter to the Galatians, he chastised some of the believers there. They had added works as a requirement for salvation in addition to what the Savior had already accomplished. Today, many Christians are still adding works to the simplicity of salvation by grace through faith! Paul warned the Colossians. Colossians 2:8:

> 8 **Beware lest any man spoil you through <u>philosophy</u> and <u>vain deceit</u>, after the <u>tradition of men</u>, after the <u>rudiments of the world</u>, and not after Christ.**

Paul's gospel message is different from that of the Twelve. In Galatians, he affirms that he did not receive it from the other apostles or from any other man. Furthermore, he affirms he received it directly from the Risen Savior. Galatians 1:11-12:

> 11 **But I certify you, brethren, that the gospel which was preached of [from] me is not after [from] man. 12 For I neither received it of man, neither was I taught it, but by the revelation of Jesus Christ.**

Growing up, I asked my Methodist pastor why he did not preach from Paul's letters. He told me that it was because Paul had persecuted the Church and, therefore, he avoided him. Another pastor told me that Paul's writings were only his opinion and therefore not reliable. Friend, either Scripture is inspired, infallible, and complete or it is not. The Bible is our only source of truth. It is authoritative and we have God's Word on it.

Paul was indeed an evil man and he admits it. He persecuted the Kingdom Believers. The following is Paul's view on this matter. Verses 13-14:

> 13 **For ye have heard of my conversation [manner of living] <u>in time past in the Jews' religion, how that beyond measure I persecuted the church of God, and wasted it</u>:**
>
> 14 **And profited in the Jews' religion above many my equals in mine own nation, being more exceedingly zealous of the traditions of my fathers.**

This is great news for people who are sinners. For if God can save Paul, then He can save anyone willing to believe. Verses 15-17:

> 15 **But <u>when it pleased God</u>, who separated me from my mother's womb, and called me by his grace, 16 <u>To reveal his Son in [to] me</u>, <u>that I might preach him among the heathen</u> [Gentiles]; immediately <u>I conferred not with flesh and blood</u> [any man]:**

17 **Neither went I up to Jerusalem to them which were apostles before me; but [instead] I went into Arabia, and [later] returned again unto Damascus.**

God set Paul apart for a special ministry to the Gentiles. This did not mean that the offer of the Gospel of Grace was not also open to the Jews. It is available to everyone but only effective for those who believe. Paul continually refers to *faith* or *the act of believing* as a requirement for salvation throughout his epistles.

Here is something that might help those new to the concept that Paul is different from the other twelve apostles. Find a large jumbo paper clip. Now, beginning with the last page of Acts and ending with the first page of Hebrews place the paper clip over those pages in between. The books within the paper clip should start with Romans and end with Philemon. They are the thirteen epistles written by Paul. You will see how this makes sense in just a moment.

In the last chapter of Acts, immediately before Paul's first book, there is a meeting recorded. It happened while Paul was incarcerated in Rome. He called the local Jewish leaders to meet with him. (See Acts 28:16-30.) After reasoning with them at great length, they remained undecided and debated amongst themselves. At this point, Paul makes a declaration which is recorded in Acts 28:28:

> **28 Be it known therefore unto you, that
> the salvation of God is sent unto the
> Gentiles, and that they will hear it.**

These are the words which end the portion of Scripture which precedes Paul's epistles. Now, let us look at the other side. If you turn to the portion of Scripture which follows Paul's epistles, the first book you come to is Hebrews. Are you starting to see a pattern here? This book of Hebrews is written to *believing Israel.* They are the Jewish believers who are following *the Gospel of the Kingdom!*

The message Paul received from the Lord Jesus Christ is directed to the Gentiles. It is called the Gospel of Grace for a reason. *Grace* means *gift* and *faith* means *believing what God said.* Therefore, salvation from this gospel message comes from believing in what God has already done for you through His Son's death, burial, and resurrection. He is graciously offering salvation as a gift to anyone who will believe. Here is the best news: Christ paid the price in full!

It is critical for our purpose to understand the two dispensations: the *Age of Law* and the *Age of Grace.* Most pastors and teachers of the Bible believe that these two dispensations are sequential meaning that one follows the other. However, this is not true. The remainder of this introduction will explain why this is so. The *Age of Law* started with Moses and was still in effect at the time of Jesus' ministry. Matthew 5:17

> 17 **Think not that I am come to destroy the law, or the prophets: I am not come to destroy, but to fulfil [the Law].**

However, Paul's message was about grace. He wrote in Galatians 2:21:

> 21 **I do not frustrate the grace of God: for if righteousness come by the law, then Christ is dead in vain.**

The *Age of Law* was temporarily suspended. It will resume once again at the close of the *Age of Grace*. This is referred to as a *parenthetical interruption*. The prophetic program given in Daniel 9 is currently in abeyance until this present age is completed. We are introduced to Paul, named Saul at that time, at the stoning of Stephen. Shortly after that, the *Age of Grace* began with the conversion of Paul. He was *the first to be saved by grace through faith*. The *Age of Grace* ends with the Rapture which the *Calling* of those saved by grace through faith.

GraceWord Publishing has excellent books which explain *rightly dividing* in greater detail. As I mentioned before, the book entitled *Letters to Theophilus* is a summary of the entire Bible from Genesis to Revelation. On the other side of the coin, *The Glorious Destiny Of Israel* presents the promises and prophecies specifically given to Israel yet to be fulfilled.

With this brief summary of the Age of Grace and Paul's unique gospel message, we are ready to begin our study of 1 & 2 Timothy and Titus.

1

About The Pastoral Epistles

We can group 1 Timothy, 2 Timothy and Titus into, what some theologians call, the pastoral epistles. Unlike Paul's other epistles, these three books, along with Philemon, are written to individuals. These three men were active in the fellowships of grace believers. Philemon was active in Colossae and the believers met in his home.

Timothy and Titus were both under the direct tutelage of the Apostle Paul. Timothy would be involved in the establishment of the believers in Ephesus. Church history records him as being the first bishop of Ephesus, although the Bible does not bestow upon him that title. Timothy, or Timotheus as he is referred to in the Bible, was actively involved with the ministry of Paul. He is mentioned several times throughout the New Testament. It was under

Paul's direction that Timothy would attain his confidence to be sent out to believers to help establish them in the faith. Titus would settle with the believers in Crete and act as an elder under Paul's supervision. This is evident in Paul's letter of instruction to him. Church history records Titus as the first bishop of Crete.

Paul was a pious Jew who, according to the Law, was blameless. Philippians 3:4-6:

> 4 Though I [Paul] might also have confidence in the flesh. If any other man thinketh that he hath whereof he might trust in the flesh, I more: 5 Circumcised [on] the eighth day, of the stock of Israel, of the tribe of Benjamin, an Hebrew of the Hebrews; as touching the law, a Pharisee;
>
> 6 Concerning zeal, persecuting the church; touching the righteousness which is in the law, blameless.

However, as the appointed Apostle to the Gentiles, he selects two subordinates who are Gentiles. In Acts, Luke writes about Timothy, his Gentile background, and his subsequent circumcision with Paul. Acts 16:1-3:

1 Then came he [Paul] to Derbe and Lystra: and, behold, a certain disciple was there, named Timotheus, the son of a certain woman, which was a Jewess, and believed; but his father was a Greek: **2** Which was well reported of by the brethren that were at Lystra and Iconium. **3** Him would Paul have to go forth [continue] with him; and took and circumcised him because of the Jews which were in those quarters: for they knew all that his father was a Greek.

Early in Paul's ministry, much of his work would involve the Jews. So as to not offend them, he had his associate Timothy circumcised to comply with the Mosaic Law. He did not do this with Titus.

Some fourteen years later after his first meeting, he met again with the Twelve. He took with him Titus who was a Gentile. Galatians 2:1-3:

1 Then fourteen years after [my first visit] I went up again to Jerusalem with Barnabas, and took Titus with me also. **2** And I went up by revelation, and communicated unto them that gospel which I preach among the Gentiles, but privately to them which were of reputation, lest by any means I should run, or had run, in vain.

3 But neither <u>Titus, who was with me, being a Greek, was compelled to be cir-cumcised</u>:

You can see Paul's ministry transitioned from a ministry to the Jew first. Romans 1:16:

16 For I am not ashamed of the gospel of Christ: for it is the power of God unto salvation to every one that believeth; <u>to the Jew first, and also to the Greek.</u>

Later, after great perseverance, his efforts being exhausted, he focuses his remaining energy on the Gentiles. Luke writes in Acts 28:28-29:

28 Be it known therefore unto you, that <u>the salvation of God is sent unto the Gentiles,</u> and that <u>they will hear it.</u> 29 And when he had said these words, the Jews departed, and had great reasoning among themselves.

These are personal letters sent to Timothy and Titus regarding the affairs of grace believer assemblies. In these epistles, Paul deals specifically with doctrine and ministry application. These letters are intended to establish guidelines by which these grace believers should govern themselves. We are now ready to begin our study.

2

1 Timothy 1

Writing to his son in the faith, Paul begins his personal letter to Timothy with this greeting. 1 Timothy 1:1-2:

> 1 **Paul, an apostle of Jesus Christ by the commandment of God our Saviour, and Lord Jesus Christ, which is our hope;** 2 <u>**Unto Timothy, my own son in the faith:**</u> **Grace, mercy, and peace, from God our Father and Jesus Christ our Lord.**

This reminds us also that our hope is *in Christ!* Everything is centered around the peace we have with God the Father. We, who were once at enmity with God, are no longer His enemies. Because of His mercy, we are saved by grace through faith in the finished work of His Son.

Timothy remained in Ephesus to continue teaching. Paul instructs him on how he should govern himself in ministering to them. Verse 3:

> 3 **As I besought thee to abide still at Ephesus, when I went into Macedonia, that thou mightest charge some that they teach no other doctrine,**

Some people seem to run off into the pucker brush and they do so unknowingly. Paul encourages Timothy to hold the believers to the true doctrine of the faith. Verse 4:

> 4 **Neither give heed to fables and endless genealogies, which minister questions, rather than <u>godly edifying which is in faith</u>: so do.**

Believers should also follow the law of love and, in loving each other, they should do so with a sincere faith. Verses 5-6:

> 5 **Now the end [purpose] of the commandment is charity out of a pure heart, and of a good conscience, and of faith unfeigned [genuine]:** 6 **From which some having swerved have turned aside unto vain jangling;**

The word *jangling* would be compared to the word *jibber-jabber* which is worthless or vain speech. To make themselves seem important, they sound authoritative and spout off their own thoughts which is vain and self-promoting.

Most of groups of grace believers were affected by Judaizers who constantly taught that the Law of Moses must be kept in addition to grace. In his letter to the Galatians, Paul deals with this extensively in the first chapter. He addresses those who want to include the Law with grace. Verse 7:

> 7 **Desiring to be teachers of the law; understanding neither what they say, nor whereof they affirm.**

Righteousness by the Law requires works of the Law. However, when it comes to salvation by grace through faith, they do not understand. Paul explains this in Romans 11:6:

> 6 **And <u>if by grace, then is it no more of works</u>: otherwise grace is no more grace. But <u>if it be of works, then is it no more grace</u>: otherwise work is no more work.**

This was a problem then and it is still a problem in

churches today. It must either be by grace or it must be by works. It is one or the other. However, for grace believers, it must be all grace!

The Law was given to the Jews for a reason. Understanding the purpose of the Law in relationship to the purpose of grace is very important. We will stop and look at what Paul wrote to the Galatians who were also trying to implement Law in addition to being saved by grace. Galatians 3:21-26:

> 21 Is the law then against the promises of God? God forbid [!]: for <u>if there had been a law given which could have given life</u>, verily <u>righteousness should have been by the law</u>.
>
> 22 But [however] the scripture hath concluded [shown that] all [are] under sin, [in order] that <u>the promise by faith of Jesus Christ might be given to them that believe</u>.
>
> 23 But <u>before faith came, we were kept under the law</u>, shut up unto [kept from] <u>the faith which should afterwards be revealed</u>.
>
> 24 Wherefore the law was our school-

master to bring us unto Christ, that we might be justified by faith.

25 But after that faith is come, we are no longer under a schoolmaster. 26 For ye are all the children of God by faith in Christ Jesus.

We are God's children by faith in the work of Jesus Christ. Friend, we are saved by *the gift of salvation* through God's Son. We accept this gift by faith which is believing what He has done for us . . . period. We must not add anything, otherwise we have another gospel which is not a gospel at all. (See Gal. 1:6-7.)

Christ did not come to abolish the Law. He came to fulfill its requirements. By fulfilling all the requirements, God could proclaim Him righteous and raise Him from the dead. It is His righteousness which God imparts to those who are *in Christ*. The moment we believe the gospel of God's grace, we are spiritually placed in His Son forever. That, my friend, is *eternal security!*

Some charge that this belief is *antinomianism* which means *against the Law*. How is this possible? Christ Himself came to fulfill the Law. Having done so, He imparted His righteousness, according to the Law, to all who, through faith, receive that righteousness as a gift? If used correctly as a guide, then the Law is good. 1 Timothy 1:8:

> 8 **But we know that the law is good, if a man use it lawfully;**

Here, the word *lawfully*, means *correctly* or *as intended*. When we sin again in the future, as sinners we certainly will, our sins are covered. Know this: they are all covered under the blood of Jesus Christ!

Now, being aware of this, we can see that the Law was intended for the unrighteous–those who are contrary to God. It is to make them aware of their sin and, most importantly, aware of their need for God's solution! Paul lists some of those for whom the Law is intended. Verses 9-10:

> 9 **Knowing this, that <u>the law is not made for a righteous man, but for the lawless and disobedient</u>, for the ungodly and for sinners, for unholy and profane, for murderers of fathers and murderers of mothers, for manslayers, 10 For whoremongers, for them that defile themselves with mankind, for menstealers, for liars, for perjured persons, and if there be <u>any other thing that is contrary to sound doctrine</u>;**

He mentions sound doctrine which is the teaching of the Gospel of Grace. This, friend, is God's solution. The Law was to make sinners aware of their need for God's righteousness! That was its purpose. Paul completes this thought with verse 11:

> 11 **According to <u>the glorious gospel</u> of the blessed God, <u>which was committed to my trust</u>.**

Notice this glorious gospel was specifically *committed to Paul*. (See Rom. 16:25.)

Paul's appointment as an apostle or messenger was made by the Lord Jesus Christ Who entrusted him with this ministry. Earlier, we read about God's specific purpose for Paul which God disclosed to Ananias. (See Acts 9:10-16.) Paul was certainly not a righteous person. He makes it clear that he is a sinner and admits it in verses 12-14:

> 12 **And I thank Christ Jesus our Lord, who hath enabled me, for that he counted me faithful, putting me into the ministry;**

> 13 **[I, Paul,] <u>Who was before a blasphemer, and a persecutor, and injurious</u>: <u>but [yet] I obtained mercy</u>, because**

I did it ignorantly in unbelief.

**14 And <u>the grace of our Lord was exceed-
ing abundant with faith and love which
is in Christ Jesus</u>.**

God showed His mercy to Paul through His grace
and overflowing love through His Son. Do you think
that God may have used Paul as an example to show
what grace can do?

If grace can be applied to Paul, once an enemy
of Jesus Christ, then this same grace can be applied
to anyone. It is important we understand this. He
calls himself the *chief* or *worst of sinners* in the verses
which follow. Verses 15-16:

> **15 This is a faithful saying, and worthy
> of all acceptation, that <u>Christ Jesus came
> into the world to save sinners; of whom
> I am chief</u>.**

> **16 Howbeit for this cause I obtained
> mercy, <u>that in me first</u> Jesus Christ
> might shew forth all longsuffering, for
> <u>a pattern to them which should hereaf-
> ter believe on him to life everlasting</u>.**

Wait just a minute! Did Paul just refer to himself as

a pattern? You might want to read the above verses again to be sure. The word *pattern* means an *example* which is to be followed. It is the first *model* or, we could say, *prototype* to be emulated or copied. Here, you have the answer if someone should ask you, "Who was the first person saved by grace?" It was Paul! In him, Christ chose to first show His mercy according to *salvation by His grace.*

Those who are saved by the Gospel of Grace should consider Paul to be their example. His life was dedicated to serving Christ. 1 Corinthians 2:2:

> 2 **For I determined not to know any thing among you, save [except] Jesus Christ, and him crucified.**

With these words, Paul is momentarily overwhelmed and glorifies God. 1 Timothy 1:17:

> 17 **Now unto the King eternal, immortal, invisible, the only wise God, be honour and glory for ever and ever. Amen.**

He returns to instructing his son in the faith. Verse 18:

> 18 **This charge I commit unto thee, son Timothy, according to the prophecies**

which went before on thee, that thou by them mightest war a good warfare;

In the above verse, *prophecies* mean *the words spoken by God.* This does not necessarily involve speaking about the future. It is the words which Timothy heard from the Apostle Paul that he must use to fight unbelief. During His testing in the wilderness following His baptism, Christ rebuffed Satan by quoting Scripture which are the words of God.

Some people did not follow instruction and, as a result, suffered the consequences. Verses 19-20:

> 19 **Holding faith, and a good conscience; which some having put away concerning faith have made shipwreck:**
>
> 20 **Of whom is Hymenaeus and Alexander; whom <u>I have delivered unto Satan, that they may learn not to blaspheme</u>.**

Their protection was temporarily removed so that they may learn a lesson. It is important to see that grace believers cannot lose their salvation because they have been bought by the blood. However, they can suffer the consequences of their actions. An alcoholic may suffer from cirrhosis of the liver. A drug addict may die from an overdose. However, their salvation is permanent. It cannot be undone.

This is such an important point, let us see Paul apply this discipline in another situation. The believers in Corinth were worldly. There was blatant sin in the assembly and the other believers were not effectively dealing with it. 1 Corinthians 5:1-5:

> 1 **It is reported commonly that there is fornication among you, and such fornication as is not so much as named among the Gentiles, that one should have his father's wife. 2 And ye are puffed up, and have not rather mourned, that he that hath done this deed might be taken [sent] away from among you. 3 For I verily, as absent in body, but present in spirit, have judged already, as though I were present, concerning him that hath so done this deed,**
>
> 4 **In the name of our Lord Jesus Christ, when ye are gathered together, and my spirit, with the power of our Lord Jesus Christ, 5 To deliver such an one unto Satan for the destruction of the flesh, that the spirit may be saved in the day of the Lord Jesus.**

Consider Paul's instructions concerning another believer who sinned. Galatians 6:1:

> 1 **Brethren, if a man [believer] be overtaken in a fault, <u>ye which are spiritual, restore such an one in the spirit of meekness;</u> considering thyself, lest thou also be tempted.**

Those who sin and continue to do so must leave the assembly. They must be allowed to suffer in their flesh the consequences of their actions. Their salvation is secure in Christ and, following repentance, should be restored to fellowship. Those who are saved by the grace of God must extend this same grace to others.

Be confident of this! Grace believers cannot lose our salvation! Our redemption has been paid in full. We have been bought with the blood of God's Son. To the church in Corinth, Paul confirms this. 1 Corinthians 6:20:

> 20 **For <u>ye are bought with a price</u>: therefore glorify God in your body, and in your spirit, which are God's.**

Friend, we must always remember this. Jesus paid it all!

3

1 Timothy 2

When we read Paul's letters, we can feel his passion. He truly cares about both his subject matter and the people to whom he is writing. At the beginning, he uses the word *exhort* which means *to use words or arguments to incite to action*. 1 Timothy 2:1:

> **1 I exhort therefore, that, first of all, supplications, prayers, intercessions, and giving of thanks, be made for all men; 2 For kings, and for all that are in authority; that we may lead a quiet and peaceable life in all godliness and honesty.**

He wants the believers to pray and intercede for all men in their conversations with God. This applies especially for those who are in leadership so that we can live our lives in peace and quiet. For this is God's intension for all mankind. Verse 3:

> 3 **For this is good and acceptable in the sight of God our Saviour;**

In the next verse, Paul discloses to us God's eternal will and purpose. Verse 4:

> 4 <u>**Who will have all men to be saved, and to come unto the knowledge of the truth.**</u>

It is God's will that *all men be saved* which applies to both men and women. How can this be done? He desires that all come to *the knowledge of the truth.* He wants everyone to hear the gospel of salvation so that they, by their freewill, can accept it. He explains *the knowledge of the truth* in verse 5:

> 5 **For there is one God, and one mediator between God and men, the man Christ Jesus;**

In the above two verses, Paul tells us what God's will is and it all centers around the Lord Jesus Christ. There are a couple of theological beliefs concerning these two verses and I would like to address them. Some Christians believe that God predetermined, in advance, those who will be saved and those who will be damned. We know that God is sovereign and it is His will that *all men be saved* (v. 4). Therefore, their position is false because God would have to contradict Himself and act contrary to His expressed will. God gave all mankind freewill so that they would love Him *by choice*. God's grace is available to all who choose to accept it once they heard it. Others are free to exercise their freewill and reject it but, in doing so, must suffer the eternal consequences. This is only possible by the free will of man. It is within the ability of all men to choose to love God or reject Him. Therefore, their destiny rests upon them and them alone.

The gift of salvation came at a great cost to God. It was the cost of His Own Son. Verses 6-7:

> 6 **Who gave himself <u>a ransom for all</u>, to be testified in due time. 7 Whereunto I am ordained a preacher, and an apostle, (I speak the truth in Christ, and lie not;) a teacher of the Gentiles in faith and verity [truth].**

Notice the words *a ransom for all*. This is important. Consider two words: sufficiency and efficiency. Sometimes the theologian in me leaks out. These are powerful words that explain something wonderful. Christ's death on the Cross is *sufficient* to save all mankind. It was enough to fulfill God's requirements for everyone. However, it is only *efficient* or effective for those who, through faith, believe in the work of His death, burial, and resurrection. (See 1 Cor. 15:1-4.) That is the Gospel of Grace.

The remaining verses of this chapter concern the conduct of grace believers within their assemblies. He begins with, what I call, meekness and modesty. Verses 8-10:

> 8 **I will [desire] therefore that men pray every where, lifting up holy hands, without wrath and doubting.**
>
> 9 **In like manner also, that women adorn themselves in modest apparel, with shamefacedness and sobriety; not with broided hair, or gold, or pearls, or costly array;** 10 **But (which becometh women professing godliness) [along] with good works.**

Many will interpret the word *broided* as meaning braided. I think it goes beyond that. The work of *embroidery* is weaving something within a cloth so as to embellish it. I believe Paul is not talking about braided, but instead weaving gold or pearls into their hair to so as to adorn themselves. Remember in all things, believers are to exercise meekness and modesty; not drawing attention to themselves. All believers must become "conformed to the image of His Son" (Rom. 8:29).

The remaining verses he devotes to the role that women are to play in the assembly. This may appear highly discriminatory, but Paul justifies his reason. Verses 11-13:

> 11 **Let the woman learn in silence with all subjection.** 12 **But I suffer not a woman to teach, nor to usurp authority over the man, but to be in silence.** 13 **For Adam was first formed, then Eve.**

His first reason is that man was created first and that woman was created from man to be his helpmeet. This created a special union to balance rationality ability of man with the woman's gift of emotions. Concerning the *original sin,* Satan first approached the woman. She felt Satan's suggestion would benefit both her husband and her, however she was deceived. Verses 14:

> 14 **And Adam was not deceived, but the woman being deceived was in the transgression.**

On this next verse, I had to ponder this a bit. I could not find any other verses using the word *childbearing*. Referring to her participation in the *original sin* mentioned above, Paul uses the word *notwithstanding* which means *nevertheless* or *in spite of this*. Then, he continues to say that she shall be saved by raising her children in faith, love, and being separated from worldliness. Verse 15:

> 15 **Notwithstanding she shall be saved in childbearing, if they [her children] continue in faith and charity and holiness with sobriety.**

God gives to women something very special. It is woman's natural response to love, care for, nurture, and raise her children to be followers of God. Each woman has the freewill to choose whether to do this or not. For those who do, God will reward them. This reward is beyond salvation because salvation is by grace through faith without works. (See Eph. 2:8-9.)

Women who teach and nurture their children in godliness will have her children blessed by God because her children are a part of her. For women, like men, are saved by grace through faith without works. Salvation is a gift offered by God and it applies to all who believe and receive it by faith.

4

1 Timothy 3

Some of this letter to Timothy concerns the administration or affairs of an assembly of believers. Having dealt with individuals, both men and women, he now turns his attention to the leadership of the assembly. He begins with the office of *bishops* or *elders* which, in the Greek, are *episkopoi* and *presbyteroi* respectively. You may recognize some words derived from these such as episcopal and presbyterian. Both of these denominations have an established hierarchy which oversees their administration.

Both the titles *bishop* and *elder* are often used interchangeably. The title *elder* may carry with it the implication of age or maturity while the title *bishop* may emphasize the charge or duty associated with their office. Some elders are teachers and preachers. Others concern themselves with the affairs of the assembly. Verses. 1 Timothy 3:1-3:

> 1 **This is a true saying, If a man desire the office of a bishop, he desireth a good work.** 2 **A bishop then <u>must be</u> blameless, the husband of one wife, vigilant, sober, of good behaviour, given to hospitality, apt to teach;** 3 **Not given to wine, no striker, not greedy of filthy lucre; but patient, not a brawler [quarrelsome], not covetous;**

We need to consider these verses carefully because they have a major impact upon the ministry of many congregations.

Notice in verse 2, Paul uses the present tense of the verb *to be*. He writes that the candidate for bishop *must be*. His use of the present tense becomes important in its interpretation. To use the present tense of *to be* means to *presently be* or *in their current state of being*. In their existing state, the candidates must meet certain qualifications. They must presently *be* blameless. Concerning Paul's past, he was not blameless. He admits that he persecuted the kingdom believers. However, now, due to the mercy and grace of God, Paul would presently *be* blameless.

Additionally, the elder must *be* married to only

one wife. He may have been married before or even had more than one wife. That was his past life. However, presently, he must *be* married to only one wife. He must *be* vigilant and sober and *be* of good behavior. If the past was held against an elder, then even the Apostle Paul would not qualify to be an elder. What happened in one's past is covered by the blood of Jesus! The qualifications which Paul lists concern the candidate's *present conversation or manner of living.*

Furthermore, the candidate must *be* hospitable. He must *be* able to teach. He must not presently *be* a drinker or someone likely to assault another. An elder must not *be* greedy for money. He must *be* patient and not someone prone to fighting with others. Finally, *having* a desire for gain or advancement *is* not acceptable. Their past sins are covered. If their sins have no impact on their relationship with God, why would Paul prevent them from leading others who *are* saved by grace? The Lord Himself, while on earth, spoke about the woman who washed His feet with her tears and dried them with her hair. Luke 7:47:

> 47 **Wherefore I say unto thee, <u>Her sins, which are many, are forgiven; for she loved much</u>: but <u>to whom little is forgiven, the same loveth little</u>.**

Much was forgiven for Paul and, therefore, he loves exceedingly. May we have more elders like Paul!

While we are discussing the qualifications of an elder,. let us stop for a moment and consider this. There is an issue in some evangelical churches and institutions concerning the translation of 1 Timothy 3:2:

> **2 A bishop then <u>must be</u> . . . the husband of one wife . . .**

Some argue the verse is about polygamy which is a man having more than one wife. They claim polygamy was not prevalent at this time even though it did exist. They interpret the text to mean that an elder cannot *be* a divorced man. To solve this conundrum, we must let Scripture provide the answer.

Consider the words of the Lord Jesus Christ in His conversation with the woman of Samaria at Jacob's well. John 4:15-18:

> **15 The woman saith unto him, Sir, give me this water, that I thirst not, neither come hither to draw. 16 Jesus saith unto her, Go, <u>call thy husband</u>, and come hither. 17 The woman answered and said, <u>I have no husband</u>. Jesus said unto**

**her, Thou hast well said, I have no hus-
band: 18 For thou hast had five husbands; and he whom thou now hast is
not thy husband: in that saidst thou
truly [answered truthfully].**

The woman told Him, "I have no husband." Knowing that she *has had* five husbands, He tells her that
she answered Him *truthfully*. He also knew that the
man she is with now *is* not her husband. She said that
she *has* no husband. The Lord agreed. This is our
proof. Men add to these requirements by reasoning
that, under the Law, the requirements must extend
to the past. The Lord disagrees. A divorce ends or
negates the former covenant requirements making it
null and void. Yes, it is sorrowful when a marriage
ends. However, the requirements of what an elder
must *be* concerns only the present. Therefore, the
candidate's past sins, like those of Paul, are forgiven.

In addition to the candidate's manner of living,
he must *be* able to manage his own affairs. In the next
verse, the translators chose the word *ruleth*. The
Greek word is *proistamenon*. It can also be translated
as *presiding over* or, more appropriately, *managing*
over his household. I say this because of the word
dispensation. The word *dispensation* comes from the
Greek word *oikonomos*. It is a compound word with
oikos meaning *household* and *nomos* meaning *law*. It is

often translated *stewardship*. A steward oversees and manages the household. The candidate should be judged on his ability to *manage* his own *household*. God chose men to act as His stewards. These men who God chose to manage His household include Adam, Noah, Abraham, and Moses. For this present dispensation, the Age of Grace, God chose the Apostle Paul.

He continues with 1 Timothy 3:4-5:

4 One that ruleth well his own house, having his children in subjection with all gravity [seriousness]; 5 (For if a man know not how to rule his own house, how shall he take care of the church of God?)

The candidate should have the ability to manage the local assembly. Verse 6:

6 Not a novice, lest being lifted up with pride he fall into the condemnation of the devil.

It is wonderful that many new converts are eager to become involved. This certainly should be encouraged. However, the role and duties of an elder require knowledge of the truth and the experience of dealing with people. As an elder, new believers might become puffed up. Therefore, Paul cautions against it. The candidate's reputation among the community, including non-believers, is important as well. Verse 7:

7 Moreover he must have a good report of them which are without [outside the assembly]; lest he fall into reproach and the snare of the devil.

He now moves on to the position of deacon. The word *deacon* comes from the Greek word *diakonos* which derives its origin meaning from *one who runs errands*. The duty of a *deacon* would not be to manage but to be a servant caring for the wellbeing of the assembly. Like the office of elder, the candidate for deacon must also meet certain expectations. Verses 8-10:

8 Likewise must the deacons be grave, not double-tongued, not given to much wine, not greedy of filthy lucre;
9 Holding the mystery of the faith in a pure conscience.

10 And let these also first be proved; then let them use the office of a deacon, being found blameless.

We might think of *double-tongued* as being two-faced saying one thing to one person and something different to another. The American Indians use to say *he who speaks with forked tongue*. In other words, deceitful. They must also *be* seasoned with experience and blameless.

In ministry, the wife of an elder or deacon has an impact on the candidate's manner of living. For that reason, the married couple should be viewed together. Verse 11:

> 11 **Even so must their wives be grave, not slanderers, sober, faithful in all things.**

Like the elder, the deacon must *be* married to one woman and *do* a good job governing his children and household. Verse 12:

> 12 **Let the deacons be the husbands of one wife, ruling their children and their own houses well.**

The next verse requires some explanation. Verse 13:

> 13 **For they that have used the office of a deacon well purchase to themselves a good degree, and great boldness in the**

faith which is in Christ Jesus.

The phrase *well purchase to themselves a good degree* may not make sense. Here is my interpretation. Consider someone who has executed or undertaken the office of deacon and done so admirably. They have *earned* the respect of the assembly. Therefore, they have *purchased* or *gained for themselves* a good reputation. This is observed by both believers and non-believers. With this, they have greater boldness in processing and teaching the faith.

It is Paul's hope to come to see Timothy again. However, if he is unable, he has given them instructions as to how he should govern himself in the affairs of the assembly. Verses 14-15:

> 14 **These things write I unto thee, hoping to come unto thee shortly: 15 But if I tarry long, that thou mayest know how thou oughtest to [you should] behave thyself in the house of God, which is the church of the living God, the pillar and ground of the truth.**

In the next verse, the word *controversy* means a *debate* or a *dispute*. He begins by saying how great is *the mystery of godliness* and it is all attributable to Christ. Verse 16:

16 And without controversy great is the mystery of godliness: God was manifest in the flesh, justified in the Spirit, seen of angels, preached unto the Gentiles, believed on in the world, received up into glory.

Look at what God has accomplished through His Son Jesus Christ. Christ was revealed in the flesh and dwelt in this world without sin among men. He was justified–being proclaimed not guilty–in the Spirit. His sinless life was witnessed by angels as proof He had fully met the requirements for the sinless sacrifice. Furthermore, Preached to the nations, which are the Gentiles, by the Apostle Paul. He is believed upon throughout the world. The Son was received by the Father in glory. In Him, as believers, we are eternally secure. He is seated in heaven with the Father and it is to this heavenly glory He will call us. We are His Body which are those saved by grace through faith!

Paul writes *great is the mystery of godliness.* What is this *mystery?* Friend, it is *the righteousness of Christ!* It is the riches of His glory. It is Christ in us, the hope of glory. Look at what Paul told the believers in Colossae. Colossians 1:25-27:

25 Whereof I [Paul] am made a minister,

according to the dispensation of God which is given to me for you, to fulfil the word of God;

26 Even [that is to say] the mystery which hath been hid from ages and from generations, but now is made manifest [known] to his saints

27 To whom God would make known what is the riches of the glory of this mystery among the Gentiles; which is Christ in you, the hope of glory:

What was once a *mystery* hidden from everyone and known only by God has now been made known. The righteousness of Christ had been given to us. Someday, we will be glorified with Him and, for us, that is *the hope of glory!*

5

1 Timothy 4

Whether in the past or present, people are always affected by strife and turmoil in the world around them. Paul uses the words *the latter times* in reference to *the last days* or *end times*. He informs Timothy of what the Spirit says will happen in these *latter days*. 1 Timothy 4:1-2:

> **1 Now the Spirit speaketh expressly, that <u>in the latter times</u> some shall depart from the faith, giving heed to seducing spirits, and doctrines of devils;**
>
> **2 Speaking lies in hypocrisy; having their conscience seared with a hot iron;**

By the end of the first century, all of the original apostles will be gone. Many who stepped into the role of apostle or teacher were self-appointed. They were not approved by God. With this came religious customs and traditions along with the vain philosophies of men. Believers would be easily seduced by *seducing spirits and doctrines of devils*. For this is the intent of the rulers of darkness. They will preach and teach lies which are hypocrisy as they are without conscience. When one's finger is seared the feeling is gone. Likewise, these servants of Satan will no longer be sensitive to the Spirit.

Exercising a counterfeit authority over their followers, they create rules and customs which are foreign to those of God. Paul lists some examples. Verses 3-5:

> 3 **Forbidding to marry, and commanding to abstain from meats, which God hath created to be received with thanksgiving of them which believe and know the truth.**
>
> 4 **For every creature of God is good, and nothing to be refused, if it be received with thanksgiving:** 5 **For it is sanctified by the word of God and prayer.**

Unlike the Jews who had dietary restrictions according to the Law, grace believers can eat as they please with thanksgiving.

Timothy is to build up grace believers by recalling for them Paul's words of faith and solid teaching. Verse 6:

> 6 **If thou put the brethren in remembrance of these things, thou shalt be a good minister of Jesus Christ, nourished up in the words of faith and of good doctrine, whereunto thou hast attained [you have already received].**

Believers are to concentrate on living godly lives and not wasting their time. They are to shun ungodly words and fables. Physical exercise may be beneficial to the body, but godliness is both valuable now and in the life to come. Verses 7-9:

> 7 **But refuse profane and old wives' fables, and exercise thyself rather unto godliness. 8 For bodily exercise profiteth little: but <u>godliness is profitable unto all things, having promise of the life that now is, and of that which is to come.</u> 9 This is a faithful saying and worthy of all acceptation.**

It is for this reason that Paul tells Timothy they both share in the work and suffer criticism. He should not feel alone in the criticism he receives.

Verse 10:

> 10 **For therefore we both labour and suf-**
> **fer reproach, because we trust in the liv-**
> **ing God, who is the Saviour of all men,**
> **specially of those that believe.**

Timothy is to use his authority to help believers to grow both by learning and doing what is taught. Verse 11:

> 11 **These things command and teach.**

Timothy had been brought up studying the Scriptures and was a quick student of Paul's teaching. When he was sent out by Paul, he was young and his youth might have been a problem for him. Paul writes concerning this in verse 12:

> 12 **Let no man despise thy youth; but be**
> **thou an example of the believers, in**
> **word, in conversation [manner of liv-**
> **ing], in charity, in spirit, in faith, in pu-**
> **rity.**

He lists aspects of the godly life which he is to exhibit to others. This includes his speech, manner of living, abundance of love for others, all while operating in the Spirit and demonstrating his faith and godliness.

Until Paul comes in person, Timothy is to concentrate on the instruction of solid Pauline doctrine. Verse 13:

13 Till I come, give attendance to reading, to exhortation, to doctrine.

He reminds Timothy he has received a gift. We should not think of the word *prophecy* as *speaking of the future*. A prophet is someone who speaks the words of God out loud so they can be heard. A preacher who preaches the Word of God could be considered a prophet. Verse 14:

14 Neglect not the gift that is in thee, which was given thee by prophecy, with the laying on of the hands of the presbytery.

Before Timothy left, as was the custom, he was sent with the laying on of hands by other elders similar to himself. This act is done by agreement of all the elders. Timothy's sending would be something they would remember as a moment in history as the confirmation of an act of God. Therefore, it was not the *presbytery* or *group of elders* who gave this gift. The gift was given by God and confirmed by spoken words from the elders. Otherwise, one might believe it was men who gave the gift.

Keeping this in memory along with knowing that the other elders, like Paul, believed in him, gave Timothy the confidence he needed. Over time, he would grow into the ministry. Verse 15:

> 15 **Meditate upon these things; give thyself wholly to them; that thy profiting may appear to all.**

In the following verse, the words *take heed* mean *pay close attention to*. Verse 16:

> 16 **Take heed unto thyself, and unto the doctrine; continue in them: for in doing this thou shalt both save thyself, and them that hear thee.**

Timothy must concentrate on teaching doctrine. There is no question that Timothy is already saved by grace through faith. Otherwise, Paul would not have approved him as a teacher of the Gospel of Grace.

As he ends, Paul makes a comparison for Timothy. He refers to his own salvation experience. In effect saying for him to concentrate on teaching sound doctrine, those who hear you will be saved in the same way you were saved–by believing the Word of God.

6

1 Timothy 5

Another word for *elder* is *overseer*. This is someone who observes and acts accordingly for the benefit of the fellowship. In the following verses, Paul uses the word *elder* to mean an *older* or *more mature* person. He gives Timothy guidance as to how an *overseer* should govern himself when interacting with believers. 1 Timothy 5:1-2:

> 1 **Rebuke not an elder, but intreat him as a father; and the younger men as brethren; 2 The elder women as mothers; the younger as sisters, with all purity.**

The fellowship of believers is a spiritual family and, in many cases, they become closer than blood relatives. He continues with verses 3-6:

3 Honour widows that are widows indeed. **4** But if any widow have children or nephews, let them learn first to shew piety at home, and to requite their parents: for that is good and acceptable before God.

5 Now she that is a widow indeed, and desolate, trusteth in God, and continueth in supplications and prayers night and day. **6** But she that liveth in pleasure is dead while she liveth.

There was no social security, government benefits program, life or disability insurance policies to provide for people. They must depend on God. What if our closeness to God was measured by our dependency upon Him? How close would we be? Those who do not depend on God miss out on the benefits of having a close relationship with Him.

A *charge* is something that is often a part of installing someone to an office or post. It is meant *to impose a duty, responsibility, or obligation* upon someone. They are *charged* fulfilling their responsibilities. Verse 7:

7 And these things give in charge, that they may be blameless.

Some members of the fellowship did not work to provide for their own living. Instead, they depended on the generosity of the others. Verse 8:

8 But if any provide not for his own, and specially for those of his own house, he hath denied the faith, and is worse than an infidel [unsaved].

However, this does not apply to a woman who has exhibited great faith in her diligence towards good works. Verses 9-10:

9 Let not a widow be taken into the number under threescore years old, having been the wife of one man,

10 Well reported of for good works; if she have brought up children, if she have lodged strangers, if she have washed the saints' feet, if she have relieved the afflicted, if she have diligently followed every good work.

On the other hand, do not extend this charity to a woman capable of working and being useful to others. Younger women who become widows can become problems. Verses 11-16:

11 But the younger widows refuse: for when they have begun to wax [grow] wanton [promiscuous] against Christ, they will marry; 12 Having damnation, because they have cast off their first faith.

13 And withal [in addition] they learn to be idle, wandering about from house to house; and not only idle, but tattlers [gossips] also and busybodies, speaking things which they ought [should] not.

14 I will [would desire] therefore that the younger women marry, bear children, guide the house, give none [no] occasion to the adversary to speak reproachfully. 15 For some are already turned aside after [to follow] Satan.

16 If any man or woman that [who] believeth have widows, let them relieve [take care of] them, and let not the church be charged [responsible]; that it [the church] may relieve them that are widows indeed [truly in need].

Elders should be honored and respected by

those in the fellowship. Paul places a special honor on those who teach. Verse 17:

17 Let the elders that rule [govern] well be counted worthy of double honour, especially they who labour in [teach] the word and doctrine.

Where providing a living wage is necessary, elders who labor in the ministry should receive a reward from the fellowship. In other words, the assembly should financially assist them. Verse 18:

18 For the scripture saith, Thou shalt not muzzle the ox that treadeth out the corn. And, The labourer is worthy of his reward.

Paul compares the work of an elder with that of an ox who works to grind the grain. The ox is free to eat from the corn he grinds. So, the support of the elder should come from the assembly.

He continues by outlining the authority of an elder. To circumvent rumors and innuendos, an elder must be accused of wrongdoing by two or three witnesses. Verse 19:

19 Against an elder receive not an accu-

sation, but before two or three witnesses.

Believers who sin should be rebuked in front of the
whole assembly so that others will fear the same. I
am confident that Paul is speaking about those who
do not listen to private admonition. Verse 20:

20 Them that [those who] sin rebuke before [in front of] all, that others also may
fear.

Everything that elders do must be done without partiality or favor. Verse 21:

21 I charge thee before God, and the
Lord Jesus Christ, and the elect angels,
that thou observe these things without
preferring one before another, doing
nothing by partiality.

Laying on of hands is a sign of partaking in
something with others. It is a sign of inclusion and,
for that reason, the other elders laid their hands upon
Timothy. Paul instructs that this be done with great
thought. For they should not lay hands on any man
too quickly and be partakers in their sins. Elders
must remain blameless and above reproach. Verse
22:

22 Lay hands suddenly [too quickly] on no man, neither be partaker of other men's sins: keep thyself pure.

On a personal note, Timothy may have suffered from a stomach issue or been prone to worry. Paul suggest that he add a little wine to his water for health reasons. Verse 23:

23 Drink no longer water [alone], but use a little wine for thy stomach's sake and thine often [your frequent] infirmities.

There are men who sin first and then others follow their example. It is for that reason that those who persist in rejecting sound doctrine must be removed from the fellowship. They cannot be allowed to continue in the fellowship while continuing to be bad examples. Likewise, those who do good works are also visible. They are seen by all and become an encouragement to others who, in turn, will emulate them. Verses 24-25:

24 Some men's sins are open beforehand, going before to judgment; and some men they follow after [them]. **25** Likewise also the good works of some are manifest beforehand; and they that are otherwise cannot be hid.

We cannot underestimate the power of our witness through our actions and words.

7

1 Timothy 6

In the final chapter of this letter, Paul continues with his instructions concerning believers. 1 Timothy 6:1-2:

> 1 **Let as many servants as are under the yoke count their own masters worthy of all honour, that the name of God and his doctrine be not blasphemed.**
>
> 2 **And they that have believing masters, let them not despise them, because they are brethren; but rather do them service, because they are faithful and beloved, partakers of the benefit. These things teach and exhort.**

Grace believers who are indentured servants to their master or under employment of their boss, must give honor to this person. If they do not, it will reflect badly upon the faith of all believers. Likewise, believing masters or bosses should not be treated with any less respect because they are believers also. For both share in the same spiritual blessings.

Should there be others in the fellowship who teach contrary to Paul's doctrine, consider their pride. Paul says that they know nothing and waste time speaking in vanity or emptiness. Verses 3-5:

> 3 **If any man teach otherwise, and consent not to wholesome words, even the words of our Lord Jesus Christ, and to the doctrine which is according to godliness;**
>
> 4 **He is proud, knowing nothing, but doting about questions and strifes of words, whereof cometh envy, strife, railings, evil surmisings,**
>
> 5 **Perverse disputings of men of [with] corrupt minds, and [yet] destitute of the truth, supposing that gain is godliness: from such withdraw thyself.**

From these corrupted believers, the true believers must withdraw themselves. How many churches can you think of that boast about their attendance or the amounts of their offerings? Think of these words: *being destitute or empty of the truth, they suppose that gain is godliness.* The *truth* is the correct interpretation of God's Word and, of this, their ministries are destitute.

Before we continue, consider what Paul wrote to the believers in Corinth. 1 Corinthians 3:19-21:

> 19 **For <u>the wisdom of this world is foolishness</u> with God. For it is written, <u>He taketh the wise in their own craftiness.</u> 20 And again, <u>The Lord knoweth the thoughts of the wise, that they are vain.</u> 21 <u>Therefore let no man glory in men</u> . . .**

In the next verse, he uses the word *contentment.* Paul teaches in Philippians that contentment is the key to happiness and "the peace of God which passeth all understanding" (Phil. 4:7) saying ". . . for I have learned, in whatsoever state I am, therewith to be content" (Phil. 4:11). He continues in 1 Timothy 6:6:

> 6 **But godliness with contentment is great gain.**

The unsaved man is like a fleeting thought or flower that blooms one day and is gone the next.

However, God endures forever. God provides and cares for believers. As such, we must not murmur, but instead be content. Verses 7-8:

> 7 **For we brought nothing into this world, and it is certain we can carry nothing out.** 8 **And having food and raiment let us be therewith content.**

Yet, the rich are tempted and often fail. Verse 9:

> 9 **But they that will be rich fall into temptation and a snare, and into many foolish and hurtful lusts, which drown men in destruction and perdition.**

Many people misquote the following verse saying that "money is the root of all evil." Actually, Scripture says something else. It says that *the love of money* is *the root of all evil.* The love of money is the cause of many heartaches. Verse 10:

> 10 **For the love of money is the root of all evil: which while some coveted after, they have erred from the faith, and pierced themselves through with many sorrows.**

Those saved by grace through faith should avoid *the*

love of money but instead seek after the things worthy of *His Calling*. Paul lists six of these traits. Verse 11:

> 11 **But thou, O man of God, flee these things; and follow after righteousness, godliness, faith, love, patience, meekness.**

The life of the believer who strives for these qualities will not be easy and it is not supposed to be. We are to bear the afflictions which Christ Himself bore while here on earth. Look at what Paul wrote in 2 Timothy 1:8-9:

> 8 **Be not thou therefore ashamed of the testimony of our Lord, nor of me his prisoner: <u>but be thou partaker of the afflictions of the gospel according to the power of God;</u>**
>
> 9 **Who hath saved us, and called us with an holy calling, not according to our works, but according to his own purpose and grace, which was given us in Christ Jesus before the world began,**

We return to 1 Timothy 6:12

> 12 **Fight the good fight of faith, lay hold**

on eternal life, whereunto thou art also called, and hast professed a good profession before many witnesses.

While we remain in our flesh here on earth, we must strive for lives of righteousness. We must hold onto the promise of eternal life *whereunto*–this is a place to which–we are also called. In the Rapture, which is the *Calling of His Body*, we are called to heaven *where* we will be with Him forever. He will appear and call those who are saved by grace to Himself. Paul speaks of our physical redemption in Ephesians 1:13-14:

> 13 **In whom ye also trusted, after that ye heard the word of truth, the gospel of your salvation: in whom also after that ye believed, <u>ye were sealed with that holy Spirit of promise</u>,**
>
> 14 **Which is the earnest of our inheritance <u>until the redemption of the purchased possession, unto the praise of his glory</u>.**

The word *earnest* is an old legal term meaning *the deposit which guarantees the completion of a transaction.* Does that mean that our bodily redemption is guaranteed? Yes, it does. We can be confident of this!

What are we supposed to do while we remain on earth waiting? Do you remember the word *charge?* It means *to impose a duty, responsibility, or obligation* upon someone. Paul makes the following *charge* before God and Christ Jesus. 1 Timothy 6:13:

> 13 **I give thee charge in the sight of God, who quickeneth [makes alive] all things, and before Christ Jesus, who before Pontius Pilate witnessed a good confession;**

Below is his *charge.* We are to be without spot or blemish. So that, at His Appearing, we will not need to be admonished. Verse 14:

> 14 **That thou keep this commandment without spot, unrebukeable, until the appearing of our Lord Jesus Christ:**

Having mentioned the Lord Jesus Christ, he elaborates upon Who He is. Verses 15-16:

> 15 **Which in his times he shall shew [will be revealed to all], who is <u>the blessed and only Potentate</u>, <u>the King of kings</u>, and <u>Lord of lords</u>;**

> 16 **Who only hath immortality, dwelling**

**in the light which no man can approach
unto; whom no man hath seen, nor can
see: to whom be honour and power ev-
erlasting. Amen.**

Many times in Paul's writings he is carried away into
words of adoration and praise. He met the Lord Jesus
face to face when he received the Gospel of Grace.
Paul, like his counterpart Moses, had a personal relationship with God. I can picture Paul dictating this
letter and, after these words of praise, I imagine him
stopping to reflect on them. These words are very
powerful. We sometimes forget our Lord Jesus is Al-
mighty God, Creator of all things.

Let us look at Colossians 1:13-14:

**13 Who [God the Father] hath delivered
us from the power of darkness, and
hath translated us into the kingdom of
his dear Son: 14 In whom we have redemption through his blood, even the
forgiveness of sins:**

He continues by painting for us a vivid picture of ex-
actly Who the dear Son of God truly is. Verses 15-18:

**15 Who is <u>the image of the invisible
God</u>, the <u>firstborn of every creature</u>:**

16 For <u>by him were all things created,</u> that are in heaven, and that are in earth, visible and invisible, whether they be thrones, or dominions, or principalities, or powers: <u>all things were created by him, and for him</u>:

17 And he is before all things, and by him all things consist. 18 And <u>he is the head of the body, the church</u>: who is the beginning, the firstborn from the dead; that <u>in all things he might have the preeminence.</u>

As grace believers, we are confident of our salvation, but do we stop to think with Whom we will spend eternity? From the moment of our salvation, we were spiritually placed *in Christ!* Now, we wait for our bodily redemption at the Rapture.

I picture Paul returning, after having thought about those words of praise, to continue his writing. He was often in prayer. He closes with these remarks to Timothy concerning the value of true riches. 1 Timothy 6:17:

17 Charge them that are rich in this world, that they be not highminded, nor trust in uncertain riches, but in the

living God, who giveth us richly all things to enjoy;

The Bible often speaks about those who are wealthy. Here, they are to be told not to trust in the *uncertainty of their earthly wealth.* They are to be told about another type of wealth. Verses 18-19:

> 18 That they <u>do good,</u> that they <u>be rich in good works, ready to distribute, willing to communicate;</u>

> 19 Laying up in store for themselves a good foundation against the time to come, that they may lay hold on eternal life.

These cannot be works to earn their salvation because they are already saved. What, then, are these riches *which shall be laid up in store for them?*

In addition to salvation, there can be so much more in heaven but it must be earned here. Paul often speaks about *rewards* for believers. We will look at several verses relating to these *rewards.* The first one makes it clear that our works are not the basis of our salvation. Romans 4:4:

> 4 Now to him that worketh is the reward

**not reckoned of [credited to] grace, but
of [to] debt.**

A worker is *owed* his wages. However, as we know, salvation cannot be earned. The *rewards* of which Paul speaks have nothing to do with salvation which, as we know, is a gift of God. I think we will see something very interesting in the following verses.

1 Corinthians 3:6-8:

> **6 I have planted, Apollos watered; but God gave the increase. 7 So then neither is he that planteth any thing, [and] neither [is] he that watereth; but God that giveth the increase.**
>
> **8 Now he that planteth and he that watereth are one: and every man shall receive his own reward according to his own labour.**

The one who plants and the one who waters are the same. They are both servants through whom the Lord works. It is clear that it is the Lord Who accomplishes the increase.

1 Corinthians 3:13-15:

13 Every man's work shall be made man-ifest [known]: for the day shall declare it, because it shall be revealed by fire; and the fire shall try every man's work of what sort it is.

14 If any man's work abide which he hath built thereupon, <u>he shall receive a reward</u>.

15 If any man's work shall be burned, <u>he shall suffer loss</u>: but he himself shall be saved; yet so as by fire.

The man whose work is tested to be good shall re-ceive a *reward*. The one who's work fails the test shall lose his *reward*. Again, this is not his salvation.

1 Corinthians 9:18-19:

18 [Paul:] <u>What is my reward then?</u> Ver-ily that, when I preach the gospel, I may make the gospel of Christ without charge, that I abuse not my power in the gospel.

19 For though I be free from all men, yet <u>have I made myself servant unto all, that I might gain the more</u>.

Colossians 3:23-25:

> **23 And whatsoever ye do, do it heartily, as to the Lord, and not unto men; 24 Knowing that of [from] the Lord ye shall receive <u>the reward</u> of the inheritance: <u>for ye serve the Lord Christ</u>.**
>
> **25 But he that doeth wrong shall receive for the wrong which he hath done: and there is no respect of persons.**

We can see that God looks upon each saved person to determine their reward. It is determined by their work and not who they are. Grace believers will receive a reward beyond their gift of eternal life. They will receive a *reward* according to the work not which they did, but according to the work they allowed Christ to do through them. I said we might find something very interesting. We should stop and think about this.

Paul ends the letter with some final instructions to Timothy. Remember and do not forget what has been taught to you. Avoid worthless or useless arguments or debates which are trifling. Notice his comment about *science* saying to avoid what is *falsely called science. Science* is the cumulative knowledge of man! Instead, we are to hold onto the true, God's Word, by our *faith*. 1 Timothy 6:20-21:

> 20 O Timothy, keep that which is committed to thy trust, avoiding profane and vain babblings, and oppositions of science falsely so called:
>
> 21 Which some professing have erred concerning the faith. Grace be with thee. Amen.

8

2 Timothy 1

Paul begins his second letter to Timothy with a salutation. In it, he reveals his fatherly relationship with him. Verses 1-2:

1 Paul, an apostle of Jesus Christ by the will of God, according to the promise of life which is in Christ Jesus, 2 To Timothy, my dearly beloved son: Grace, mercy, and peace, from God the Father and Christ Jesus our Lord.

He expresses his gratitude to God for having a fellow worker such as Timothy with which to work in the ministry of the Gospel of Grace. Verses 3-4:

3 I thank God, whom I serve from my forefathers with pure conscience, that without ceasing I have remembrance of

thee in my prayers night and day;

4 Greatly desiring to see thee, being mindful of thy tears, that I may be filled with joy;

He longs to see him knowing the trials and afflictions Timothy is facing. Paul had brought salvation to Timothy and enlisted him in the service of the Lord. For that reason, he often refers to him as his son in the faith. Timothy had a mother and grandmother who were women of faith. Verse 5.

5 When I call to remembrance the unfeigned faith that is in thee, which dwelt first in thy grandmother Lois, and thy mother Eunice; and I am persuaded that in thee also.

It appears from some of his writing that Timothy was either frail or timid in his demeanor. If that is the case, he would be an excellent example of someone who allowed the Lord to work through him in His ministry. God said to the Apostle Paul, ". . . for My strength is made perfect in weakness" (2 Cor.12:9). Let us continue with verses 6-7:

6 Wherefore I put thee in remembrance that thou stir up the gift of God, which

is in thee by the putting on of my hands.

7 <u>For God hath not given us the spirit of fear; but of power, and of love, and of a sound mind</u>.

Paul had laid hands on Timothy as part of his acceptance into the ministry. He reminds Timothy, as one saved by grace, he is not to be fearful. We are to be confident, able to love, and not be easily confused.

Timothy should be neither embarrassed nor ashamed of the gospel message or of Paul who is a prisoner of the gospel. As someone who has studied the God-given temperaments, Timothy has a passive and task-oriented temperament. In other words, he is a deep thinker. If this is the case, he must rely on God to provide him with the necessary skills and abilities to do what Paul is asking of him. Verses 8:

8 Be not thou therefore ashamed of the testimony of our Lord, nor of me his prisoner: but <u>be thou partaker of the af-flictions of the gospel</u> according to the power of God;

Let us consider the words *partaker of the afflictions of the gospel* as they have specific meaning. Redemption occurs in three stages. The first is when we are saved and spiritually placed in Christ Who is in heaven. The second stage deals with our flesh or body. Our body remains on earth as we await the completion of our redemption. The process of sanctification, I believe, is a process completed by God. Paul writes in Philippians 1:6:

> **6 Being confident of this very thing, that he which hath begun a good work in you will perform it until the day of Jesus Christ:**

The day of Jesus Christ is the Rapture. During our time on earth, we are awaiting the final stage of our redemption–our glorification. All who are waiting, we will suffer in this world. Look at what Paul wrote in Romans 8:16-18:

> **16 The Spirit itself beareth witness with our spirit, that we are the children of God: 17 And if [His] children, then heirs; heirs of God, and joint heirs with Christ; <u>if so be that we suffer with him, that we may be also glorified together</u>.**
>
> **18 For I reckon that <u>the sufferings of this present time</u> are not worthy to be compared with the glory which shall be revealed in us.**

This is important! Our torments and afflictions that we suffer in this world are because we are His children. Our sanctification is the process of being separated from the world. Yet, there is good news. Notice verse 17 says we *suffer with Him* so that we can also be *glorified together* with Him! Having just mentioned *God*, he continues with this doctrinal statement. 2 Timothy 1:9:

> 9 **Who hath saved us, and called us with an holy calling, <u>not according to our works</u>, <u>but according to his own purpose and grace</u>, <u>which was given us in Christ Jesus</u> before the world began,**

The salvation of each individual was not predetermined. The purpose and final destination of those who accept God's gracious gift by faith was predetermined before the world began.

He continues by expounding upon what is now in effect starting with the revelation of the mystery given to Paul. Verses 10-11:

> 10 **But is now made manifest [known] by the appearing of our Saviour Jesus Christ, who hath abolished death, and hath brought life and immortality to light through the gospel:**

11 **Whereunto <u>I am appointed a preacher, and an apostle, and a teacher of the Gentiles</u>.**

This agrees with what he wrote to the believers in Romans 16:25:

25 **<u>Now</u> to him that is of power to stablish you <u>according to my gospel,</u> <u>and the preaching of Jesus Christ,</u> <u>according to the revelation of the mystery,</u> which was kept secret since the world began,**

Paul's gospel is unique. He is the Apostle to the Gentiles according to the direct appointment by God. (See Rom. 11:13.)

Paul states that he is to be an example to Timothy as well as all grace believers. Throughout all his sufferings, he trusts in God. He reamins confident that his sanctification, which he has committed to God, will be completed by Him. 2 Timothy 1:12:

12 **For the which cause <u>I also suffer these things</u>: nevertheless I am not ashamed: for <u>I know whom I have believed</u>, and am persuaded that <u>he is able to keep that which I have committed unto him</u> against [upon] that day.**

Paul trusts his sanctification is in the hands of God. When will it be completed? God will complete it upon *that day* in which Christ calls to Himself all grace believers. It is *the Day of our Lord Jesus Christ!* See 1 Corinthians 1:7-8:

> **7 So that ye come behind in no gift; <u>waiting for the coming of our Lord Jesus Christ:</u>**
>
> **8 <u>Who shall also confirm [complete in] you unto the end,</u> that ye may be blameless in <u>the day of our Lord Jesus Christ</u>.**

Friend, the doctrines we are studying here are not *milk!* They are for those who are mature in the Lord. Paul's doctrine is *meat!* Do not be concerned if you have not heard them taught before. I have found that many preachers give a sermon which is *topical*. This means they choose a portion from Scripture and then present other verses related to that subject. This book is an *expositional* commentary. This means I am constrained to teach the Bible verse by verse. I may use other verses to expound on the current verses, but I cannot skip the primary text. In this case, the text is the books of Timothy and Titus.

I recommend after you complete this commentary, you go back and read the books directly from the Bible. Each Christian, like the noble Bereans, should consider what is being said, then go to the Scripture to see if what was said is so. (See Acts 17:10-11.) When you read more of Paul's epistles, you will find the important concepts which we discuss here will be confirmed over and over again. The more you read them, you will find for yourself that you understand them better and begin to commit them to memory. Think about this. What Paul is teaching should cause great joy for all grace believers! Christ has saved us. Christ is sanctifying us. And, at *the day of our Lord Jesus Christ*, He will glorify us to be forever with Him! Hallelujah!

Looking at other epistles of Paul, we see a common theme. He prays for grace believers that they all receive the same thing. See if you can pick out what is the common theme among them.

Romans 11:33:

> 33 O <u>the depth of the riches both of the wisdom and knowledge of God!</u> how unsearchable are his judgments, and his ways past finding out!

Ephesians 1:17-18:

> 17 That the God of our Lord Jesus Christ,

the Father of glory, <u>may give unto you</u> <u>the spirit of wisdom and revelation in</u> <u>the knowledge of him</u>:

18 The <u>eyes of your understanding</u> be-ing enlightened<u>; that ye may know</u> <u>what is the hope of his calling</u>, and <u>what</u> <u>the riches of the glory of his inheritance</u> <u>in the saints</u>,

Colossians 1:9:

9 For this cause we also, since the day we heard it, do not cease to pray for you, and to desire <u>that ye might be filled</u> <u>with the knowledge of his will in all</u> <u>wisdom and spiritual understanding</u>;

Colossians 2:2-3:

2 That their hearts might be comforted, being knit together in love, and unto <u>all</u> <u>riches of the full assurance of under-</u> <u>standing</u>, to <u>the acknowledgement of</u> <u>the mystery of God</u>, and of the Father, and <u>of Christ</u>;

3 <u>In whom are hid all the treasures of</u> <u>wisdom and knowledge</u>.

The central theme of these verses is Paul's desire that grace believers come to full knowledge, wisdom, and understanding. Where are these treasures of *wisdom and knowledge* hidden? All of them can be found *in Christ*.

So, they are found *in Christ*. How do we get them? Look at the Gospel of John 1:1-2:

> 1 **In the beginning was the Word, and the Word was with God, and the Word was God.** 2 **The same was in the beginning with God**

Here it is, my friend. Christ is the *Word of God*. The *Word of God* is the Bible. Therefore, everything Paul wants us to know is found in the *Word of God—the Bible!* There is *milk* for new believers and there is *meat* for those who are mature. Right now, we are being fed meat!

The last portion of his instruction has to do with teaching and holding onto foundational doctrine. Timothy was taught directly by Paul. 2 Timothy 1:13-14:

> 13 **Hold fast the form of sound words, which thou hast heard of [from] me, in faith and love which is in Christ Jesus.**

14 That good thing which was committed unto thee keep by the Holy Ghost which dwelleth in us.

The Holy Spirit plays a vital role in Scripture. He inspired its writers and, when someone reads it, the Holy Spirit illuminates its meaning to those who seek to understand it. When studying Scripture, it is best to ask the Author for help in understanding the Word of God. You can tell Him that Paul sent you.

He ends this chapter with some personal notes. Verses 15-18:

15 This thou knowest, that all they which are in Asia be turned away from me; of whom are Phygellus and Hermogenes. 16 The Lord give mercy unto the house of Onesiphorus; for he oft refreshed me, and was not ashamed of my chain [being in prison]:

17 But, when he was in Rome, he sought me out very diligently, and found me. 18 The Lord grant unto him that he may find mercy of the Lord in that day: and in how many things he ministered unto me at Ephesus, thou knowest very well.

In the above closing remarks, there is something I would like to bring to your attention. He tells Timothy that he knows *that all they which are in Asia be turned away from me.* This has great theological import. In the first chapter of Revelation, John records the words of the Lord Jesus Christ concerning the seven churches in Asia. They are Ephesus, Smyrna, Pergamos, Thyatira, Sardis, Philadelphia, and Laodicea. These were churches in the first century, in Paul's time, that were located in Asia Minor or present-day Turkey. Revelation 1:20:

> 20 **The mystery of the seven stars which thou sawest in my right hand, and the seven golden candlesticks. The seven stars are the angels of <u>the seven churches</u>: and <u>the seven candlesticks which thou sawest are the seven churches</u>.**

When Paul speaks of these churches turning from him, he is referring to them leaving his teaching, abandoning sound doctrine. This is the same thing of which he warns Timothy. One might raise a question. We are told that all grace believers will be saved, sanctified, and glorified by the Lord Jesus Christ. This is correct. Yet, we find these same churches, where Paul taught, are in Revelation and being judged. So, what is up with that? It has to do with the warning which

Paul gave to Timothy above. 2 Timothy 1:13:

13 <u>Hold fast the form of sound words</u> <u>[doctrine],</u> which thou hast heard of [from] me, in faith and love which is in Christ Jesus.

Like the Galatians who turned to another gospel, which was not a gospel at all, these other assemblies departed from Paul's teaching. They added to or revised the Gospel of Grace to their own peril.

Grace believers are forgiven. They have the righteousness of Christ impressed upon them. How, then, can they be judged? They cannot! These churches in Asia had left Paul's teaching, Their salvation was not by grace through faith without works. By the time of their judgment in Revelation, they were following the Gospel of the Kingdom and they were doing a poor job at that. For a deeper explanation of this consider reading *Letters To Theophilus — Are You Ready For The End Times?*

9

2 Timothy 2

We can only presume from what we see in ministry today that Timothy was weary from the opposition he was experiencing. The ministry of the Gospel of Grace was new and he was one of the first who followed in Paul's footsteps. We know that he had been taught and was capable. Otherwise, he would not have been sent to Ephesus by Paul. It is to this young teacher, he writes verses 1-2:

> 1 **Thou therefore, my son [in the faith], be strong in the grace that is in Christ Jesus. 2 And the things that thou hast heard of [from] me among many witnesses, the same commit thou to faithful men, who shall be able to teach others also.**

As mentioned, the opposition made the teaching of the gospel difficult. We find these words of explanation in Ephesians 6:12:

> 12 **For we wrestle not against flesh and blood, but against principalities, against powers, against the rulers of the darkness of this world, against spiritual wickedness in high places.**

Therefore, this spiritual battle is going on and Timothy is unknowingly a participant. 2 Timothy 2:3-4:

> 3 **Thou therefore [are to] endure hardness, as a good soldier of Jesus Christ.**

> 4 **No man that warreth entangleth himself with the affairs of this life; that he may please him who hath chosen him to be a soldier.**

Now, engaged in this battle, he should not get *entangled* or *caught up in* other matters but rather remain focused on the purpose for which he was chosen remembering by Whom he was sent.

This applies to anything one seeks to master whether it be a profession or ministry. Below, Paul uses the word *strive*. This means to *exert much effort, fight vigorously, or contend with conviction*. Verse 5:

5 And if a man also strive for masteries, yet is he not crowned [a victor], except he strive lawfully.

As an example, he uses the husbandman who tends a vineyard to maximize his harvest. Verses 6-7

6 The husbandman that laboureth must be first partaker of the fruits. **7** Consider what I say; and the Lord give thee understanding in all things.

The fruits are the benefits of the husbandman's harvest. Paul is telling Timothy that he must enjoy the benefit of understanding himself before he can share it with others.

He returns to coaching Timothy by recalling those things which he has already taught him concerning the Christ. Verses 8-10:

8 Remember that Jesus Christ of the seed of David was raised from the dead according to my gospel: **9** Wherein I suffer trouble, as an evil doer, even unto bonds [being arrested]; but the word of God is not bound.

10 Therefore I endure all things for the

elect's sakes, that they may also obtain the salvation which is in Christ Jesus with eternal glory.

Even while Paul was imprisoned in Rome awaiting his trial, he continues to diligently work for the furtherance of the gospel. He endures much opposition himself, but he strives so that the message would not be bound like he was.

Most believers saved by grace have found that teaching or explaining the grace message is difficult. The message itself is quite simple, but those willing to hear it are few. Then, there is the opposition of powers and principalities, rulers of darkness. However, there is great consolation which he writes about in Romans 8:37-39:

37 Nay, in all these things we are more than conquerors through him that loved us.

38 For I am persuaded, that neither death, nor life, nor angels, nor principalities, nor powers, nor things present, nor things to come, 39 Nor height, nor depth, nor any other creature, shall be able to separate us from the love of God, which is in Christ Jesus our Lord. [!]

He offers us consolation with our future destiny in the Lord Jesus Christ. 2 Timothy 2:11-13:

> 11 **It is a faithful saying:** <u>**For if we be dead with him, we shall also live with him:**</u>
>
> 12 <u>**If we suffer, we shall also reign with him:**</u> **if we deny him, he also will deny us:** 13 **If we believe not, yet he abideth faithful: he cannot deny himself.**

With all that we have received and will receive, we cannot deny the Lord.

He tells Timothy to stop believers from wasting their time arguing about minute details which is unprofitable. For by doing that, it subverts or negatively impacts those who are listening. The word *subvert* means *to overthrow, undermine,* or *render ineffective.* This is not to be the purpose of believers but to make known the good news of the gospel. Verse 14:

> 14 **Of these things put them in remembrance, charging them before the Lord that they strive not about words to no profit, but to the subverting of the hearers.**

So, subverting hearers would be contrary to growing the group of believers.

The following verse is one of those that is the hallmark verse for understanding the Bible dispensationally. Therefore, it is not directed to Timothy alone, but to all who want to understand God's Word. No one wants to be ashamed or embarrassed by incorrect interpretation. Verse 15:

> 15 **Study to shew thyself approved unto God, a workman that needeth not to be ashamed, <u>rightly dividing the word of truth</u>.**

I think of *rightly dividing the Word of Truth*, or the Word of God, as not crossing over lines. What was given to one does not apply to another. We know that all Scripture was written *for us*. Paul confirms this in the next chapter in 1 Timothy 3:16:

> 16 **All scripture is given by inspiration of God, and is profitable for doctrine, for reproof, for correction, for instruction in righteousness:**

However, during this current Age of Grace, it is only the writings of Paul, the Apostle to the Gentiles, which specifically apply *to us*.

He continues his discussion of useless speech. By using the word *profane,* he means *irreverent, showing contempt for the sacred, or polluted speech.* An example would be taking the Lord's name in vain. If it is not stopped, then it will grow. 2 Timothy 2:16-18:

> 16 **But shun profane and vain babblings: for they will increase unto more ungodliness.**
>
> 17 **And their word will eat as doth a canker: of whom is Hymenaeus and Philetus;**
>
> 18 **Who concerning the truth have erred, saying that the resurrection [Rapture] is past already; and overthrow the faith of some.**

Citing the examples of two individuals and comparing their words as a canker or cancer. They were wrong in their beliefs and were saying that the Rapture had already occurred. This heresy made some believe they had lost hope for the resurrection.

Irrespective of any heresies, the doctrine of God still stands and He knowns his own. Verse 19:

19 **Nevertheless the foundation of God**

standeth sure, [and] having this seal [upon them], The Lord knoweth them that are his. And, Let every one that nameth the name of Christ depart from iniquity.

Paul uses the word *vessel* which is *an item used to carry or contain something* such as a pitcher. He goes on to explain there are many vessels in a great house. How they are used by the master of the house depends upon the vessel. Verse 20:

20 But in a great house there are not only vessels of gold and of silver, but also of wood and of earth; and some to honour, and some to dishonour.

He now applies this to a man who is himself a *vessel* that carries something. Verse 21:

21 If a man therefore purge himself from these, he shall be a vessel unto honour, sanctified, and meet [acceptable] for the master's use, and prepared unto every good work.

As mature believers, things from their youth must be put away and replaced with fruits of the spirit which are worthy. Verses 22-23:

22 Flee also youthful lusts: but follow righteousness, faith, charity, peace, with them that call on the Lord out of a pure heart.

23 But foolish and unlearned questions avoid, knowing that they do gender [cause] strifes [conflicts].

The grace believer who seeks to serve the Lord must have the following attributes. Verse 24:

24 And the servant of the Lord must not strive; but be gentle unto all men, apt [able] to teach, patient,

Remember that it is God's will or desire ". . . to make all men see what is the fellowship of the mystery . . ." (Eph. 3:9). For this reason, Paul continues with verses 25-26:

25 In meekness instructing those that oppose themselves; if God peradventure [perhaps] will give them repentance to the acknowledging of the truth; **26** And that they may recover themselves out of the snare of the devil, who are taken captive by him [the devil] at his will.

Paul's desire for both Timothy and Titus, as fellow laborers in the field, is to reach more of the lost that they too may be saved by grace through faith. Both had heard Paul teach. Now, they are to take the Gospel of Grace, teach it well, and commit it to ". . . faithful men, who shall be able to teach others also" (2 Tim. 2:2).

10

2 Timothy 3

When we read the following verses we cannot help but put this into the context of present-day geopolitics. We must remember these words were written by the Apostle Paul almost two thousand years ago. We can understand how believers at that time would have felt when someone told them the Rapture had already happened. This left them without *the blessed hope* of bodily redemption before the Tribulation. In view of today's events, I am confident the Rapture is imminent.

He writes about the *last days* and what believers can expect. 2 Timothy 3:1-4:

> 1 **This know also, that in the last days perilous times shall come. 2 For men shall be lovers of their own selves,**

covetous, boasters, proud, blasphemers, disobedient to parents, unthankful, unholy,

3 Without natural affection, truce-breakers, false accusers, incontinent, fierce, despisers of those that are good, 4 Traitors, heady, high-minded, lovers of pleasures more than lovers of God;

Most of these we know. I have a passion for works and was curious to understand the word *heady*. It means *intoxicating or stupefying.* In other words, people will be acting as if they were drunk or stupid. To this, I can add nothing.

He continues with those who, by appearances, are believers, but really they are not. Verses 5-7:

5 Having a [an outward] form of godliness, but denying the power thereof: from such turn away.

6 For of this sort are they which creep into houses, and lead captive silly women laden with sins, led away with divers [different] lusts,

7 Ever learning, and never able to come

to the knowledge of the truth.

Appearing to be friends and harmless, they worm their way into people's lives unnoticed. They are disguised as righteous, but they deny the power of God. *Silliness* is *a weakness of understanding or lack of sound judgment.* At this time, women are home alone all day. They are easy prey to be led away from the truth. Men strive to achieve greater science or knowledge, but they never attain knowledge of the truth of God. Look around. Do we see any of this happening today?

Paul was a Pharisee. This is the same as having a doctorate in the Jewish religion. He refers to the two magicians or sorcerers of Pharoah. These two enchanters counterfeited the miracles of Moses in Exodus chapter 7 and 8. However, they could not duplicate everything! Verses 8-9:

> 8 **Now as Jannes and Jambres withstood Moses, so do these also resist the truth: men of corrupt minds, reprobate concerning the faith.**
>
> 9 **But they shall proceed no further: for their folly shall be manifest [made known] unto all men, as theirs [Jannes and Jambres] also was.**

Most, if not all, public displays of miracles today are not of God. They are performed by those having *a form of godliness* and yet counterfeit the power thereof. Eventually, like Jannes and Jambres, they too will become unmasked. From them, turn away!

Timothy was well acquainted with Paul having spent much time together hearing him teach. Verse 10:

> 10 **But thou hast fully known my doctrine, manner of life, purpose, faith, longsuffering, charity, patience,**

He was also aware of Paul's sufferings. Verse 11:

> 11 **Persecutions, afflictions, which came unto me at Antioch, at Iconium, at Lystra; what persecutions I endured: but out of them all the Lord delivered me.**

In telling Timothy, Paul tells us that all believers who live a life worthy of *His Calling* will experience suffering. Verses 12-13:

> 12 **Yea, and all that will live godly in Christ Jesus shall suffer persecution.** 13 **But <u>evil men and seducers shall wax [grow] worse and worse, deceiving, and</u>**

being deceived.

As grace believers await their *Calling*, they will witness the growth of evil. Many preachers today teach that it is the believers who will bring in the Kingdom. Believers must all work for the Kingdom! They believe they will eventually save the world and usher in the King! How foolish. This is a lie and the true essence of humanism! Only the Lord can save. Paul is saying there will be more and more who deceive others and an increase of those who are deceived themselves.

Paul encourages Timothy to remain steadfast and hold onto what he was taught. As a child, he was brought up in a home where they studied Scripture. Upon hearing the Gospel of Grace preached by Paul, he believed and was saved by faith. Verses 14-15:

> 14 **But continue thou in the things which thou hast learned and hast been assured of, knowing of whom thou hast learned them;**
>
> 15 **And that from a child thou hast known the holy scriptures, which are able to make thee wise unto salvation through faith which is in Christ Jesus.**

Paul ends his letter to Timothy by stressing the importance of Scripture and the importance it plays in salvation and upon the lives of believers. Scripture is trustworthy because it is inspired. It is God-breathed. God Himself is its Author. Verses 16-17:

16 **All scripture is given by inspiration of God, and is profitable for doctrine, for reproof, for correction, for instruction in righteousness:**

17 **That the man of God may be perfect, thoroughly furnished unto all good works.**

11

2 Timothy 4

How would we define the word *charge?* In the following context, it means *laying the responsibility for a task or duty upon a person.* It is often used as part of an installation to a particular position. Paul charges Timothy before God and Christ as witnesses. 2 Timothy4:1:

1 I charge thee therefore before God, and the Lord Jesus Christ, who shall judge the quick [living] and the dead at his appearing and his kingdom;

Notice that it is the Lord Jesus Christ who will judge the living and the dead at both His Appearing and when His Kingdom is established.

Here is what Timothy must do. Verse 2-4:

2 Preach the word; be instant in season, out of season; reprove, rebuke, exhort with all longsuffering [patience] and doctrine. 3 For the time will come when they will not endure sound doctrine; but [instead seeking] after their own lusts shall they heap to themselves teachers, having itching ears; 4 And they shall turn away their ears from [listening to] the truth, and shall be turned unto fables.

Paul wants Timothy to continue to proclaim the gospel in spite of his afflictions. He must also persevere. Verse 5:

5 But watch thou in all things, endure afflictions, do the work of an evangelist, make full proof of thy ministry.

He is to endure the opposition as he shares the good news. There is an old English saying: "the proof is in the putting" or in the doing. Someone can present the concept of rightly dividing the word of truth, but until it is sufficiently tested, a novice will still need proof. At this point in my life, I have personally tested interpreting Scripture dispensationally for seven years. I have made *full proof* that rightly dividing Scripture, without a doubt, is totally correct. (See 2 Tim. 2:15.)

Paul has been under house arrest in Rome awaiting his trial before Caesar. Nero Claudius Caesar August Germanicus is responsible for putting Paul to death. Nero is the emperor of the Roman Empire from 54 AD to 68 AD. Most historians date Paul's death in 68 AD. Aware that his death was imminent, we can sense it in his writing. Verses 6-8:

> 6 **For I am now ready to be offered, and <u>the time of my departure is at hand</u>.** 7 **I have fought a good fight, I have finished my course, I have kept the faith:**
>
> 8 **Henceforth there is laid up for me a crown of righteousness, which the Lord, the righteous judge, shall give me at that day: and <u>not to me only, but unto all them also that love his appearing</u>.**

Paul is confident he will receive his reward from the Lord. He will receive it when his body is called at *the day of the Lord Jesus*–the Rapture. Likewise, grace believers who also await His Appearing will receive their rewards as well.

Eager to have Timothy visit him, he desires to see him face to face before his *departure*. Paul asks him to do whatever is necessary to make it happen. He has been deserted by all except Luke who still remains. He tells Timothy to bring Mark with him. So that the Ephesians would not be without a teacher, Paul sends Tychicus to replace him. Verses 9-12:

> 9 **Do thy diligence to come shortly unto me:** 10 **For Demas hath forsaken me, having loved this present world, and is departed unto Thessalonica; Crescens to Galatia, Titus unto Dalmatia.**

> 11 **Only Luke is with me. Take Mark, and bring him with thee: for he is profitable to me for the ministry.** 12 **And Tychicus have I sent to Ephesus.**

Now aged, Paul is suffering from the cold and asks for his cloak, his books, and some parchments to write additional letters. He remains active in service to God until his death. Verse 13:

> 13 **The cloke that I left at Troas with Carpus, when thou comest, bring with thee, and the books, but especially the parchments.**

He mentions some of his opposition. Paul does not seek vengeance but trusts that the Lord will deal with them appropriately. Verses 14-15:

> 14 **Alexander the coppersmith did me much evil: the Lord reward him according to his works: 15 Of whom be thou ware [beware of] also; for he hath greatly withstood our words.**

At his first appearance in Caesar's court, Paul was there alone. Verse 16:

> 16 **At my first answer no man stood with me, but all men forsook me: I pray God that it may not be laid to their charge.**

Do you remember the words God spoke to Ananias? Acts 9:15-16:

> 15 **But the Lord said unto him, Go thy way: <u>for he is a chosen vessel unto me, to bear my name before the Gentiles, and kings,</u> and the children of Israel: 16 For <u>I will shew him how great things he must suffer for my name's sake</u>.**

Now, he is at the end of his life and everything that the Lord God said He would do with Paul, He will accomplish.

Although he stood alone, the Lord stood with him. Paul was emboldened to proclaim the Gospel of Grace before Caesar. He wanted it to be a testimony for God. For him, it was always about Christ alone. He once said, "For I determined not to know anything among you, save [except] Jesus Christ, and Him crucified" (1 Cor. 2:2). 2 Timothy 4:17:

> 17 **Notwithstanding the Lord stood with me, and strengthened me; that by me the preaching might be fully known, and that all the Gentiles might hear: and I was delivered out of the mouth of the lion.**

He compares his situation with the prophet Daniel who withstood the lions because God was also with him. He is confident that the Lord will deliver him from *every evil work*. Verse 18:

> 18 **And the Lord <u>shall deliver me from every evil work</u>, <u>and will preserve me unto his heavenly kingdom</u>: to whom be glory for ever and ever. Amen.**

One might ask, "But, Paul dies. How can God preserve him until the Rapture?" Regardless of his physical state, God will deliver him to an eternal life in the heavens. Paul confirms this in 2 Corinthians 5:6-8:

> **6 Therefore we are always confident, knowing that, <u>whilst we are at home in the body, we are absent from the Lord</u>: 7 (For we walk by faith, not by sight:)**
>
> **8 <u>We are confident, I say, and willing rather to be absent from the body, and to be present with the Lord</u>.**

We too, like Paul, can join in praise to God *to Whom be glory for ever and ever. Amen!*

He adds some comments and greetings to his personal acquaintances as he closes. 2 Timothy 4:19-20:

> **19 Salute Prisca and Aquila, and the household of Onesiphorus.**
>
> **20 Erastus abode at Corinth: but Trophimus have I left at Miletum sick.**

Thinking of that cloak, he reminds Timothy that it would be great if he came before winter. Some additional greetings are added. Verse 21:

21 Do thy diligence to come before winter. Eubulus greeteth thee, and Pudens, and Linus, and Claudia, and all the brethren.

Then, he concludes with this blessing meant specifically for Timothy using the singular pronoun *thy spirit.* Verse 22:

22 The Lord Jesus Christ be with thy spirit. Grace be with you. Amen.

12

Titus 1

Like Timothy, Titus is also a student of Paul and learned directly from him. A fellow laborer with the Gospel of Grace, Paul writes this letter to him. He begins by proclaiming his own apostleship. Titus 1:1:

1 Paul, a servant of God, and an apostle of Jesus Christ, according to the faith of God's elect, and the acknowledging of the truth which is after godliness;

He continues by writing about our hope of eternal life with God. This *mystery* was revealed to Paul who is the Apostle to the Gentiles. It was committed to Paul by the Risen Savior. Verses 2-3:

2 In hope of eternal life, which God, that [Who] cannot lie, promised before the world began;

3 <u>But hath in due times</u> manifested his word through preaching, which is <u>committed unto me according to the commandment of God our Saviour;</u>

Titus, like Timothy, is viewed by Paul as a "son" in the faith which they now share. To this, he adds his apostolic blessing. Verse 4:

4 To Titus, mine own son after the common faith: Grace, mercy, and peace, from God the Father and the Lord Jesus Christ our Saviour.

Titus is on the beautiful island of Crete which is located south of Greece in the Mediterranean Sea. Paul stopped there on a missionary trip. The island is large enough to include mountains while being set in an azure sea. It was once home to ancient civilizations, but it is now part of the Roman Empire. Titus had remained there to establish the believers in the same manner as Timothy remained in Ephesus. Verse 5:

5 For this cause [reason] left I thee in Crete, that thou shouldest set in order the things that are wanting, and ordain elders in every city, as I had [also] appointed thee:

The *elder* or *overseer* plays an important role in establishing a permanent assembly. Similar to his letter to Timothy, he restates several of the requirements for a candidate of *elder*. Verses 6-9:

> 6 **If any [man] be blameless, the husband of one wife, having faithful children not accused of riot or unruly.** 7 **For a bishop [elder] must be blameless, as the steward of God; not self-willed, not soon angry, not given to wine, no striker, not given to filthy lucre;**

> 8 **But a lover of hospitality, a lover of good men, sober, just, holy, temperate;** 9 **Holding fast the faithful word as he hath been taught, that he may be able by sound doctrine both to exhort and to convince the gainsayers.**

A *gainsayer* is *someone who contradicts, denies or opposes* what is being taught. An *elder* must not only know doctrine but he should also be able to defend it.

He describes potential opposition that an elder must handle properly. Verses 10-11:

> 10 **For there are many unruly and vain [self-centered] talkers and deceivers,**

specially they of the circumcision
[Jews]:

**11 Whose mouths must be stopped, who
subvert whole houses, teaching things
which they ought not, for filthy lucre's
[money's] sake.**

One of the Jews who was a prophet and a native Cretian was speaking derogatorily of the inhabitants of Crete. He calls them liars, evil, and lazy. Paul does not deny it, but they must be rebuked. They must confine themselves to sound teaching and not political commentary. Verses 12-13:

**12 One of themselves [one of the Cretians], even a prophet of their own, said,
The Cretians are alway liars, evil beasts,
slow bellies. 13 This witness is true.
Wherefore rebuke them sharply, that
they may be sound in the faith;**

Crete had a colony of Jewish merchants and traders for centuries. So, there were many Jews who were living on the island. Verse 14:

**14 Not giving heed to Jewish fables, and
commandments of men, that turn from
the truth.**

A *fable* is an *invented story or tale* which is intended for instruction or amusement. Regardless, it is not the truth. If someone is a believer or not, then it will impact their thoughts and their actions. For example, an atheist will see the world from a completely different perspective than someone who follows God. They have come to their own beliefs and conclusions which are foreign to believers. Verse 15-16:

> 15 **Unto the pure all things are pure: but unto them that are defiled and unbelieving is nothing pure; but even their mind and conscience is defiled.**

> 16 **They profess that they know God; but in [their] works [actions] they deny him, being abominable, and disobedient, and unto every good work reprobate.**

To reach these people, someone must take on the role of an apologist. This is a person who has sufficient knowledge of the Bible to defend it.

The role of elder, bishop, or pastor is not an easy one. He must have the necessary knowledge and experience to handle diverse situation. The man who takes on this role must be exemplary knowing sound doctrine. He must be able to teach it and refute those who oppose it. Finally, he must be able to properly handle the varied groups of people with whom he will interact. Recall what Paul wrote to Timothy concerning elders in 1 Timothy 5:17:

> 17 Let the elders that rule [govern] well be counted worthy of double honour, especially they `who labour in the word and doctrine.

13

Titus 2

The words from an elder are heard by both believers and non-believers. May they be considered worthy and of sound doctrine which is foundational truth. Titus 2:1:

1 But speak thou the things which become sound doctrine:

Instruction of the believers goes beyond doctrine to include its proper application as well. Paul addresses the various people within an assembly and gives his expectations. He begins with men and women of maturity. Verses 2-5:

2 That the aged [mature] men be sober, grave, temperate, sound in faith, in charity, in patience.

3 The aged [mature] women likewise, that they be in behaviour as becometh holiness, not false accusers, not given to much wine, teachers of good things;

4 That they may teach the young women to be sober, to love their husbands, to love their children, 5 To be discreet, chaste, keepers at home, good, obedient to their own husbands, that the word of God be not blasphemed.

He addresses the young men who will someday enter leadership in the assembly and their community. Verses 6-8:

6 Young men likewise exhort to be sober minded. 7 In all things shewing thyself a pattern of good works: in doctrine shewing uncorruptness, gravity, sincerity,

8 Sound speech, that cannot be condemned; that he that is of the contrary part [unbelievers] may be ashamed, having no evil thing to say of you.

Paul himself was to be a *patten*. (See 1 Tim. 1:16.) These young meny are to imitate Paul and, thereby, be a pattern to others.

At the time this letter was written, slaves and servants comprised a large part of the population. Today, we can apply this to employer-employee relationships. Verses 9-10:

> 9 **Exhort servants to be obedient unto their own masters, and to please them well in all things; not answering again;**
>
> 10 **Not purloining [stealing], but shewing all good fidelity [faithfulness]; that they may adorn the doctrine of God our Saviour in all things.**

The phrase *that they may adorn the doctrine of God our Saviour in all things* may be interpreted this way. May the quality, care, and diligence of their work radiate the glory of God's teaching.

The message of the Gospel of Grace was received by the Apostle Paul with instructions by the Risen Lord to carry that message faithfully. Some people take words from what is being taught and then misuse them. Paul instructs that his words must be repeated faithfully. Paul seeks to instruct faithful men with his message and he hopes they will also follow his example. Let us look again at what he wrote in 2 Timothy 2:2:

> 2 **And the things that thou hast heard of [from] me among many witnesses, the same commit thou to faithful men, who shall be able to teach others also.**

He summarizes what he committed to Titus by writing Titus 2:11-14:

> 11 **For the grace of God that bringeth salvation hath appeared to all men,**
>
> 12 **Teaching us that, [1] denying ungodliness and worldly lusts, [2] we should live soberly, righteously, and godly, in this present world; 13 [3] Looking for that blessed hope, and the glorious appearing of the great God and our Saviour Jesus Christ;**
>
> 14 **Who gave himself for us, that he might redeem us from all iniquity, and purify unto himself a peculiar people, zealous of good works.**

The following are Paul's expectations for Titus. Verse 15:

15 **These things speak, and exhort, and rebuke with all authority. Let no man [have cause to] despise thee.**

As the Apostle of the Gospel of Grace, Paul wants his teaching to be repeated faithfully and without change. His doctrine still remains the basis of faith and living for believers. Grace believers continue today to wait with great expectation for His Appearing. At that moment, Christ will appear and call us, those saved by grace through faith without works, unto Himself.

14

Titus 3

Paul gives Titus some practical application of his doctrine. This is how he wants grace believers to act while they wait for *His Calling*. Titus is to teach and exhort the assembly on what is appropriate. Titus 3:1-2

> 1 **Put them in mind [Remind them] to be subject to principalities and powers, to obey magistrates, to be ready to [do] every good work,**
>
> 2 **To speak evil of no man, to be no [not] brawlers, but gentle, shewing all meekness unto all men.**

Believers are to follow the laws of the land and be respectful of those in authority. They are not to be rabble rousers or rebellious against the government.

He reminds Titus that they were both once unsaved, disobedient, and an enemy of God. Verse 3:

> 3 **For we ourselves also were sometimes foolish, disobedient, deceived, serving divers lusts and pleasures, living in malice and envy, hateful, and hating one another.**

However, while all of us were still sinners, Christ died for us. (See Rom. 5:8.) No one earns or deserves their salvation. It is a gift from God. Verses 4-5:

> 4 **But after that the kindness and love of God our Saviour toward man appeared,**
>
> 5 **Not by works of righteousness which we have done, but according to his mercy he saved us, by the washing of regeneration, and renewing of the Holy Ghost;**

It is God's Son Who paid the price for our salvation. Not only did He justify us, but He also made us co-heirs with Christ. Verses 6-7:

> 6 **Which he shed on us abundantly through Jesus Christ our Saviour; 7 That being justified by his grace, we should**

be made heirs according to the hope of eternal life.

We need to take a moment and look at this concept of being heirs. As Paul's letter to Titus is a summary and instruction on applying doctrine, Titus is well aware of the teachings of Paul. Here are several verses which will help us understand the concept of *the inheritance* of the believers.

Romans 8:14-17:

> 14 **For as many as are led by the Spirit of God, <u>they are the sons of God</u>.** 15 **For ye have not received the spirit of bondage again to fear; but <u>ye have received the Spirit of adoption</u>, whereby we cry, Abba, Father.**
>
> 16 **The Spirit itself beareth witness with our spirit, that <u>we are the children of God</u>:** 17 **<u>And if children, then heirs; heirs of God, and joint-heirs with Christ</u>; if so be that we suffer with him, that we may be also glorified together.**

Galatians 3:26:

> 26 **<u>For ye are all the children of God</u> by**

117

faith in Christ Jesus.

Ephesians 1:12-14:

12 That we should be to the praise of his glory, who first trusted in Christ.

13 In whom ye also trusted, after that ye heard the word of truth, the gospel of your salvation: in whom also after that ye believed, ye were sealed with that holy Spirit of promise, 14 Which is the earnest [deposit] of our inheritance until the redemption of the purchased possession [the Rapture], unto the praise of his glory.

Ephesians 1:18:

18 [Paul prays that] The eyes of your understanding being enlightened; that ye may know what is the hope of his calling [the Rapture], and what the riches of the glory of his inheritance in the saints,

Colossians 1:12:

12 Giving thanks unto the Father, which hath made us meet [acceptable] to be

partakers of the inheritance of the saints in light [glory]:

Colossians 3:24:

> 24 **Knowing that of the Lord ye shall receive the reward of the inheritance: for ye serve the Lord Christ.**

Friend, this is such wonderful news! How much more is this than our salvation! We can understand why Paul often bursts into words of praise in his writing.

Having reminded Titus of these foundations of our salvation and hope, he resumes his instruction. Titus 2:8:

> 8 **This is a faithful saying, and these things I will that thou affirm constantly, that they which have believed in God might be careful to maintain good works. These things are good and profitable unto men.**

Those who have a true heart for God are almost compelled to do something to serve Him. The works are a fruit or yield of a vibrant and active faith. These works are not to attain salvation which is secure for all believers. For our salvation has been paid in full by the blood of Jesus Christ and the redemption of His purchased possession is guaranteed by the Holy Spirit. (See Eph. 1:13-14.) Instead, we are actually allowing the Spirit, Who is within us, to serve God through us.

With such an important message to proclaim, Paul warns against wasting time. Verse 9:

> 9 **But avoid foolish questions, and genealogies, and contentions, and strivings about the law; for they are unprofitable and vain.**

With the latter days quickly approaching all diligence must be made to make known the gospel of our salvation. However, should someone within the assembly be belligerent in opposing the teaching, this person should be removed. This would be after gentle and repeated admonishing. By rejecting sound teaching, they condemn themselves. Verses 10-11:

> 10 **A man that is an heretick [heretic] after the first and second admonition reject;** 11 **Knowing that he that is such is subverted, and sinneth, being condemned of himself.**

120

Paul plans on sending a substitute teacher to allow Titus to come to him. Nicopolis is a city located on the western side of Greece on the Ionic Sea. There, he plans to spend the winter. Not being very far by ship, he requests that Titus visit him there. Verses 12-14:

12 **When I shall send Artemas unto thee, or Tychicus, be diligent to come unto me to Nicopolis: for I have determined there to winter.**

13 **Bring Zenas the lawyer and Apollos on their journey diligently, that nothing be wanting unto them.**

14 **And let ours also learn to maintain good works for necessary uses, that they be not unfruitful.**

There are two others which he request Titus bring with him so that he may review with them their teaching. Paul was ever vigilant that the doctrine being taught was correct.

He ends his letter with this salutation in verse 15:

15 **All that are with me salute thee. Greet**

them that love us in the faith. Grace be with you all. Amen.

Epilogue

Paul, the Apostle of the Gospel of the Grace of God, received his gospel from the Risen Savior. (See Eph 3:1-2.) It was a constant concern for him that the information he taught was not being changed by others. Since the very beginning, it has been Satan's goal to corrupt the truth of God.

How are believers to know what the truth of God really is? There is no need to be concerned because He has written everything down for us. Not only has He written it, He has also preserved it. Therefore, for those who love Him, we must study to show ourselves approved so that, as believers, we will not be embarrassed by incorrectly interpreting God's Word. We must rightly divide the word of truth. (See 2 Tim. 2:15.) All of Paul's epistles carry the same message. His message never changed.

This book includes three of Paul's letters often referred to as *the pastoral epistles*. These were written to younger teachers in the faith who needed extra guidance and encouragement. They are the source of information for those considering and appointing leadership within an assembly. There is a lot to consider when realizing the importance of leadership. It affects both the effectiveness of the ministry as well as the spiritual health of the fellowship of believers.

Dr. David Alan Greene

Other GraceWord Publications

Cartas A Teófilo
Efesios: Dispensacionalmente considerado
El evangelio Oculto: Una vez fue un misterio . . .

About The Author

Dr. David Alan Greene has over thirty-five years of experience as an insurance agent selling both property and casualty as well as life insurance. During his career, he taught and explained the content and meaning of policies to his clients. Now retired, he devotes much of his time to teaching the Bible.

He obtained his Bachelor of Theology, Master of Biblical Studies, and Ph.D. in Biblical Studies from Evangelical Theological Seminary where he holds the position of Dean of Graduate Studies. He also holds a Ph.D. in Christian Counseling. He has written numerous biblical commentaries and books on rightly dividing the Word of Truth.

www.ingramcontent.com/pod-product-compliance
Lightning Source LLC
Chambersburg PA
CBHW060826120626
46557CB00001B/393